LOST HISTORY OF STOLEN CHILDREN

AN EPIC POEM

Being a true accounting of white children

kidnapped and sold into slavery

at the Chesapeake Bay and the Delaware River

in the seventeenth century

and what became of them afterwards

ANNOTATED EDITION

by Richard Hayes Phillips, Ph.D.

It cost me a lot of hard work to get this into verse.

Copyright © 2019 by Richard Hayes Phillips
4 Fisher Street, Canton, New York, 13617
All rights reserved

First Printing
2019

LIBRARY OF CONGRESS CATALOGING-IN-PUBLICATION DATA
Phillips, Richard Hayes, 1951-
Lost History of Stolen Children: An Epic Poem

1. History -- 17th century   2. Slavery -- Maryland – Virginia -- Pennsylvania
3. Kidnapping -- Ireland -- Scotland -- England -- New England   I. Title

First printing with Annotations

Published by
Genealogical Publishing Company
Baltimore, Maryland
2021

Copyright © 2021 by Richard Hayes Phillips
4 Fisher Street, Canton, New York, 13617
All rights reserved

ISBN 9780806321158

PREFACE

THE WRITING OF THE POEM

At the eleventh hour on New Year's Eve, 2017, I stretched out on my sofa with three translations of *The Odyssey*, deciding which one to read. It was required reading when I was in middle school, but I had not read it since then.

Suddenly it dawned on me: I have both the skills and the material to write an epic poem. Not as long as *The Odyssey*, perhaps, but certainly as long as the epic poems of Longfellow.

I am a long-time songwriter and folksinger in the Scottish and Irish tradition. And I have compelling stories of children whose survival itself was heroic.

There was no decision to begin. The first two lines came to me right away. Before long I had the whole first passage. What was difficult was making the commitment to continue.

I had already published three history books about white children kidnapped from England, Scotland, Ireland, and Massachusetts and sold into slavery in Maryland and Virginia. * I knew their names and their ages. In many cases I knew the shires and counties from which they were taken, how they were treated during their years in bondage, and what became of those who survived the ordeal. The challenge would be to transform these stories, with historical accuracy, into lyric poetry, with rhyme and meter.

As with any investigation, I would reexamine the evidence and follow any leads that might appear. I found records of children kidnapped from Scotland and sold into slavery in Pennsylvania. I tracked the movements of runaways and their descendants through the Appalachian Mountains. I found more shipping records identifying the captains of the ships that transported them. And I searched newly available parish records to identify more of the parents.

It soon became apparent that I would need to publish an annotated version of the epic poem, in order to prove it is all true. In most instances I could cite my own books. Oftentimes I would need to elaborate on how I arrived at my conclusions. And I would need to provide all of my new material in a companion volume, a supplement to my published trilogy of history books.

And so I compiled the new evidence into book format as I went along, and meticulously organized all of my source material into hundreds of file folders that would enable me to find it later, when the epic poem was completed, and the time came to write the annotations. This book is the result.

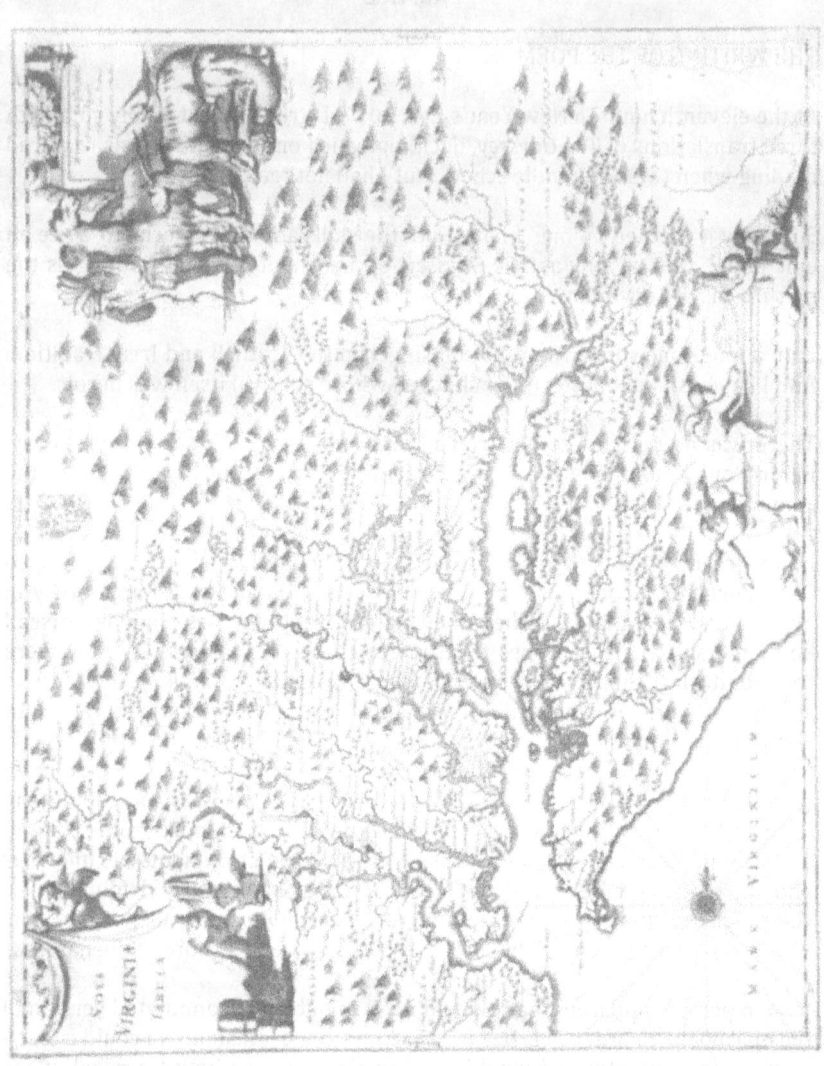

Map of Chesapeake Bay, 1671, rotated so that north is at the top. Kidnapped children were trapped on peninsulas, in between rivers. Ships could sail inland to the Fall Line, where the rivers descended from the foothills onto the coastal plain. Beyond this was wilderness, where the homesteads were few and remote, and runaways were safely beyond the long arm of the law.

PART ONE

I.

Truth is an elusive thing; its trail will soon grow cold,
Especially if someone does not want it to be told.
It may be on the record, and written down in books,
But none will ever know of it if no one cares to look.

Some books are lost in fires, or eaten up by worms;
Some are shelved for centuries, their pages never turned
Until, at last, one looks upon what long had been concealed,
For there is nothing hidden that will not be revealed.

Truth is everlasting, immutable, eternal.
The story may survive intact if written in a journal;
But if passed down by word of mouth, some will not believe it.
Once the legend is forgotten there is no way to retrieve it.

And then what cannot be explained is in the realm of mystery,
For none alive remember what was once well known as history.
We pretend it did not happen if we do not like the story,
For we prefer inspiring myths of righteousness and glory.

The shining city on the hill. I hear that phony story still,
And I suppose I always will, it seems to give them such a thrill.
Our founders sailed across the sea, inspired by God and liberty,
Set up a state where all are free, and passed it down to you and me.

Not all at once; we have our stains. The Africans were brought in chains,
Found freedom only in the grave, but only these were ever slaves.
Indentured servants came at will. They worked for years to pay the bill
Of passage on the sailing ship, for they could not afford the trip.

But this was simply not the same. The whites were never brought in chains,
Unless convicted of a crime, transported here to serve their time.
We fought a war, the blacks are free, with equal opportunity.
That is how I learned the song. But now I know they got it wrong.

When searching family history of three centuries ago,
I came upon a story that nobody seemed to know,
About a Scottish family, ancestors of mine,
Ten long generations before the present time. [8]

II.

One day in late September David Hambleton was slain
On the river that they called Newichawannock,
That forms the western border of the present State of Maine,
By Algonquins who would hunt and fish upon it.

He was born in Westburn, Lanarkshire, upon the River Clyde,
A bit southeast of Glasgow in the lowland countryside.
His father was an old man but he knew, before he died,
To instill his little Davie with a sense of Scottish pride.

He was kin to Scottish royalty, to all the Stewart kings,
Dating back to Bruce the Liberator.
When Cromwell seized the Parliament, and overthrew the king,
The Hambletons viewed Cromwell as a traitor.

David was a young man at the onset of the war.
He had to fight, he saw his duty clearly.
He bade farewell to Annah Jaxson, the little girl next door,
Who was far too young to wed, but loved him dearly.

At Worcester he was taken as a prisoner of war,
And shipped to North America in chains,
And sold for thirty pounds to be a slave forever more
At a saw mill on the rocky coast of Maine.

But when the mill went bankrupt all the prisoners were freed,
And David built a house with his own hands,
And after years of struggle he at last obtained a deed,
And became the legal owner of the land.

He sent for Annah Jaxson for to sail across the foam,
To marry him and cherish him forever.
Eight young sons she bore him in their little wooden home
On the banks of the Newichawannock River.

But the both of them were killed, and they died without a will,
And the orphans' house and land were handed over
Not for public use, but to a private speculator
By officials of the nearby Town of Dover.

The youngest boy was James, and they shipped him off in chains,
A specimen of value, strong and braw.
They sent him to Virginia from the rocky coast of Maine,
And made him "serve according to the law."

He sometimes came to court and demanded to be freed,
But his master and the court were unrepentant.
They stripped him and they whipped him for the words he dared to speak,
And added extra years onto his sentence.

Fourteen years he labored in the hot Virginia sun,
Pulling stumps and harvesting tobacco,
Until at last they freed him at the age of thirty-one,
As under English common law they had to.

In twelve more years he had enough tobacco for to buy
A hundred acre homestead of his own.
Both James and Grace, his wife, were in their forties when they died,
And they never saw their children fully grown.

Three hundred years have come and gone; no remnants have survived,
No traces of this family can be found,
But a monument to David high above the riverside,
And his stone foundation deep beneath the ground. [21]

III.

Such cryptic words: that he must "serve according to the law."
Just what law that might be was not disclosed.
I searched the laws of Maryland and Britain and Virginia,
To find out what I never had supposed.

It was sixteen fifty-nine, just after Cromwell died,
And the Stewarts not yet back upon the throne,
When the House of Commons made the law on which the court relied,
Authorizing children to be taken from their homes.

It was lawful for a constable or justice of the peace
To capture any vagrant, begging child,
Convey them unto any port, and place them on a ship,
Without a court appearance or a trial,

And send them overseas to colonial plantations
Where the landed gentry launched their latest ventures,
To labor for the wealthy, the established aristocracy,
As nothing more than slaves without indentures.

An indenture is a contract, a voluntary thing,
Written down on paper, signed and witnessed.
But these were kidnapped children taken quite against their will,
And the merchants saw it all as strictly business.

What consigned these kids to slavery, having no indentures,
Was an order from the judges who examined them.
"Gentleman Justices" they called them in Virginia,
And "Worshipful Commissioners" in Maryland.

Their owners who had bought them from the captain, or at auction,
Brought them into court, and the judges guessed their ages.
The sentences were set by law; the youngest got the longest,
And their Christian names were written on the pages. [28]

IV.

It wasn't only James. There were many other names
On the record on a single day in sixteen ninety-nine.
The oldest one was eighteen years. The youngest ones were nine.
And I began to wonder just how many I could find.

So I took a train to Fredericksburg, and hitchhiked forty miles
To the county in the Northern Neck where James had been a slave.
One Court Order Book was lost; the others had been saved.
I found three hundred kidnapped children, long forgotten in their graves.

This was just Westmoreland County. There were many other counties
Where most of the Court Order Books had managed to survive.
I found that in Virginia many books had been transcribed,
And in Maryland I learned to read the writing of the scribes.

My hands would tingle every time I touched the pages,
As I searched within a book so very old.
My eyes would cry whenever I would see the ages
Of the little ones whose tales had not been told.

And I could almost hear their voices crying:
"Please be careful, do not miss my name,
It is written in that book, no one else will ever look,
I have waited for so long, find my name."

Some of those Court Order Books had never once been opened
Since the scribes had put the books away three hundred years ago.
In all I found five thousand names that no one cared to know.
They were hidden in plain sight. I wondered how this could be so.

None who came before me had ever found the story.
Books had been transcribed, and typewritten, word for word,
Yet no one ever thought about the wording that they saw,
Or wondered what it meant to "serve according to the law." [35]

V.

I could not help but notice. There were fifteen hundred children
Whose owners all were justices who sat upon the bench,
So they had a vested interest in continuing the system,
And all the while pretending to be Christians.

Imagine what it felt like to be shipped across the ocean,
Chained below the deck, with the waves in constant motion,
Not knowing why they captured you, or where you might be going,
With your father and your mother never knowing.

The ship sails into port in a place you've never been,
And then the captain sells you to a man you've never seen,
Who drags you into court where the judges are his friends,
And they sentence you to slavery. The nightmare never ends.

The traffic in white children peaked in sixteen ninety-nine,
With nearly seven hundred of them listed at that time.
One day in Talbot County there appeared one hundred four,
And on the next day there were fourteen more.

Negro children also would appear before the court.
There were thirteen, in eight counties, in sixteen ninety-nine.
Three years later there were fifty, and the whites were forty-nine.
I would later learn the reason for the timeline.

Almost never were these victims allowed to tell their tales.
I wondered where they came from, the ports from which they sailed,
The shires or counties of their birth, and where they were baptized.
I wanted to know something of their lives.

I hadn't much to go on, but I had a little bit.
Four hundred sixty children had identified the ships.
If I could find the shipping records my knowledge would be larger,
For I would know the ports of departure. [42]

VI.

Sometimes the name of the ship was a clue
Containing the place name of where it was from.
And there would be more than I already knew.
I didn't have all, but I surely had some:

Whitehaven, Derry, and Dublin,
Bridgwater, Belfast, and London,
Bideford, Plymouth and Topsham,
Bristol, and somewhere in Scotland.

So I flew into Dublin, and traveled around,
Looking for records in every port town.
I would find a mere page, or would utterly fail,
Till I crossed on a ferry from Ireland to Wales.

They sheltered me there, for a night, from the rain.
From Pembroke to Bristol I rode on the train.
I rode into Somerset, Hampshire, and Devon,
And found little more than I had when I came.

I rode back to Bristol, and everything changed.
The old shipping records were neatly arranged
For twenty-eight years harking back to the days
When children were shipped to the Chesapeake Bay.

Twenty-four ships that were harbored at Bristol
Turned out to be some of the same
One hundred and twenty-five ships that were named
In the Court Order Books of the Chesapeake Bay.

The records at Bristol did not state the cargo,
But none of the passenger lists had the names
Of the children who had no indentures
When brought before court in the Chesapeake Bay.

Some who were bound for Virginia and Maryland
Stopped in New England before they were through,
And two of the ships were from Boston,
Suggesting that kids had been captured there too.

I later found records in Scotland and Boston.
From Glasgow and Edinburgh, down at the quay,
Commencing their trips were the very same ships
That were named by the children at Chesapeake Bay.

Sailing from Scotland, with owners in Boston,
Or sailing from Bristol, or chartered in London,
All tied together in one great endeavor:
Shipping the children to Chesapeake Bay. [52]

VII.

I never did make it to London.
I hadn't the money, I hadn't the time.
I wanted the records from Chesapeake Bay
If by chance there were any to find.

I expected no records from Maryland.
I had asked about these once before.
They were lost in a fire at the State House
In seventeen hundred and four.

But at the Library of Congress
They reached for a book from the shelf,
An index to duplicate records from London,
And told me to search for myself.

And under the heading of "Shipping"
One single entry appeared,
Ending in seventeen hundred and two,
Which included the very peak years.

They were black and white photostat copies,
Oversize and in high resolution,
Of one hundred handwritten ledgers.
It took me two days to get through them.

For every ship passing through Maryland ports,
Not always, but often, the records would show:
The name of the ship, and where it was built,
And where it had come from, and where it would go,

The date of arrival, the date of departure,
The name of the captain, the names of the owners,
The taxes they paid, and to whom, on the cargo.
I suddenly had what I needed to know.

Forty-five slave ships that had not been named
By the kids in the Chesapeake courts,
Were newly revealed by the cargo they carried
Or duties they paid at the ports.

A tax of two shillings and six pence was paid
On every child they imported.
They were not referring to African slaves.
"European" is what was reported.

They never recorded a name,
But only the number that came.
They were openly listed as cargo,
Along with the rum and tobacco.

Nine hundred and seven were brought in one year.
The ledgers recorded the cost.
The stories of many have long disappeared
Where the Court Order Books have been lost.

From Whitehaven, Liverpool, Bristol and Bideford,
Derry and Belfast, Dublin and Cork,
Newcastle, Falmouth, Plymouth and London,
Sixty-eight ships sailed to Maryland ports.

And this was in thirteen years' time.
I still had the records from everywhere else.
I had names of one hundred and seventy ships
Counting everything found on the shelf.

And now I knew seventeen ports of departure.
Perhaps I could find where the children were from.
A targeted search of the baptismal records
Wouldn't find all, but would surely find some.

For I knew the real names of the children,
And I knew their approximate ages.
If I searched for a name in the proper time frame,
And it showed only once on the pages

Of any birth record from churches or towns
Near the ports where the children were taken,
I could match the birth parents with disappeared child,
And probably not be mistaken.

Some of the children would never be found
If the court books omitted their ages,
Or were damaged by water, or eaten by worms,
Or the corners were gone from the pages,

Or the scribe had too horribly mangled the name,
Or the handwriting wasn't sufficiently clear,
Or if two or more kids with the very same name
Had been born in about the same year.

The birth records, also, would not be complete,
Although I would search far and wide.
Historians know to accept what is lost,
And be grateful for what has survived. [71]

VIII.

In the port of Dublin, in nineteen twenty two,
Stood the building they call the Four Courts.
The Public Records Office was the west wing
Where centuries of manuscripts were stored.

Church and court papers from the Middle Ages,
Deeds and wills from three hundred years before,
Military records from the eighteenth century,
Transportation records with pleas for clemency,

All the census records up to eighteen fifty one --
The demographic record of the famine,
Parish records dating to the seventeenth century,
Are lost, never more to be examined.

It happened in the battle over Irish independence.
In the treaty that was signed, these terms were written:
The so-called Irish Free State would not be fully free
But would remain within the Commonwealth of Britain.

Such autonomy was more than Ireland had before the war,
And the signers could defend what they agreed to,
But some had lost their lives fighting for the Irish side,
And no one could have seen what this would lead to.

The anti-treaty forces occupied the Four Courts
And used the archives to store their ammunition.
They knew that Irish history rested in their hands.
But they would not abandon their position.

Armed with rifles and machine guns,
They would not be the first ones to fire.
They turned the Four Courts into a fortress
With sand bags, trenches, mines, and barbed wire.

Stationed in Dublin were six thousand British troops
To enforce all the terms of the treaty.
The Free State forces would attack the Four Courts,
And the British would provide the artillery.

The Free State forces surrounded Four Courts,
Gave the occupiers twenty minutes warning.
The cannons commenced the bombardment
At four o'clock in the morning.

The siege went on for three nights and three days
Till fires broke out in the building,
And spread till they reached the ammunition,
Causing an explosion in the west wing.

A thick black cloud two hundred feet high
Drifted away in the wind,
And fluttering about like sea gulls
Were the leaves of white paper within.

Centuries of history were totally destroyed.
The loss is lamented to this day.
If this is the cost of independence,
'Tis a price we should not have had to pay. [83]

IX.

I wanted to see every church and town record
From counties or shires of departure,
But reason dictated to focus my search
Where the rates of return would be larger.

From seventeenth century Ireland
Only ten parish records survived
From Derry and Belfast, Dublin and Cork,
And these, long ago, were transcribed.

For both Massachusetts and Scotland,
The records were posted online,
And also for Cheshire and Lancashire,
So these were quite easy to find.

But there were so many more people in London,
Back then it was four hundred thousand,
And from Essex and Kent, downstream on the Thames,
Where they loaded the ships at the port of Gravesend,

Only part of the records were posted online,
There were too many missing, and not enough time
For one lone historian, doing his best,
To search for, and find, and examine the rest.

So I focused instead on the west coast of England,
On Cumberland, Devon, and Gloucester,
Where the records online were substantial enough
That one man could finish the roster. [89]

X.

If you go to Whitehaven, in the shire of Cumberland,
Stand upon the strand, look upon the Irish Sea,
Listen to the waves lapping on the Old Quay,
And contemplate the way it used to be.

It was built in days of yore, in sixteen thirty four,
With a beacon on the pier, and a small house made of stone.
See the moss upon the sides. You can almost hear the cries
Of children who went missing from their homes.

It was once a holding cell for captive children,
As young as six years old, so very small.
And if they let you look inside the windows,
The iron cuffs are still upon the walls.

They were waiting to be shipped to the plantations,
To be slaves till they were more than fully grown.
Their only crime was to be looked upon as vagrants.
The constables could seize them on their own.

Amid the pounding of the surf, look across the Solway Firth,
See the snow-capped Southern Uplands of Scotland.
How this image must have lingered in the hearts and minds
Of these helpless kids that time has long forgotten.

Walk along the Coastal Path, looking downward as you pass,
At the sea cliffs at your feet, and the rocky shores below.
Imagine panicked children escaping down the cliffs
Where the constables, they knew, could never go.

The dock upon the sea was the exciting place to be.
Children liked to watch the ships sail in.
And suddenly, one day, they would be spirited away.
They never knew the danger they were in.

The Nightingale, the Ruby, the Loves Increase, the Charity,
The Charles, and the Thomas, as the shipping records show,
Sailed out of Whitehaven, to Virginia or to Maryland,
With European "servants" as their "Cargo."

These were not servants with indentures.
Most of them were too young to sign one.
But if kidnapped and conveyed to the Chesapeake Bay,
The courts had the power to bind one.

If you go to Whitehaven, in the shire of Cumberland,
Stand upon the strand, look upon the Irish Sea,
Listen to the waves lapping on the Old Quay,
And contemplate the way it used to be. [99]

XI.

Who were the traffickers, the financiers,
Whose investments got it all started,
Who built their fortunes, and all profiteered
On the backs of the broken hearted?

The Planters Adventure was a London ship.
Carried kids to Virginia on at least six trips.
Thirty-one kids identified the ship
In the courts of York or Middlesex County.

Nathaniel Bacon was the President
Of the Virginia Council of the State.
George Poindexter and Otto Thorpe
Stole land and timber from orphans' estates.

John Page was a colonel in the army of the king
And a member of the House of Burgesses.
Three of the four were on the York County Court
That sentenced these children to service.

The Duke of York had been a Navy ship.
Carried kids to Virginia on at least eight trips.
Twenty-two kids identified the ship
In Lancaster, York, or Middlesex County.

All four of the owners served on the Court
Of Middlesex County, Virginia.
And one of these was Sir Henry Chicheley,
The Governor of Virginia.

All eight owners of these two ships,
The Duke of York, and the Planters Adventure,
Between them owned at least sixty-seven
Children without indentures.

The Planters Adventure carried kids from London
And from Scotland, Cheshire, and Devon.
The Duke of York carried kids from London
And from Gloucester, Lancashire, and Dublin.

The Concord of London was a Navy ship.
Carried kids to Virginia on at least five trips.
The first was in sixteen seventy-five,
The fifth in sixteen eighty.

Seventeen kids identified the ship
In the court books of York County.
Sir Thomas Grantham commanded the ship
While still in the service of the Navy.

The Concord sometimes sailed from Bristol,
Carrying kids from Gloucester and Devon.
And who would be the owner of a Navy ship?
King Charles the Second. [110]

XII.

Slavery had long been sanctioned by the Stuart kings.
James the First sent three hundred kids to Jamestown,
Taken by the constables, off the London streets.
Sad to say, they never wrote the names down.

In the year of sixteen sixty, after Charles gained the throne,
The Privy Council heard about the ships upon the Thames,
How children, every day, were taken up, enticed away,
At the ports of London and Gravesend,

To be shipped away and sold in West Indies or Virginia,
To labor for the merchants and the planters,
"Crying and mourning for redemption from their slavery,"
If ransom was not paid to the Commander.

Calling it "Kidnapping," they ordered Customs Officers
To board and search the vessels, and to set the children free,
And to bring before the Council anyone who would resist,
But nothing ever came of this decree.

The Royal African Company, founded sixteen sixty,
By James, Duke of York, the king's brother,
Took control of the trades for gold and for slaves,
A monopoly by law, there were no others.

These were all London ships, and they limited the trips,
To three thousand slaves from Africa per year,
And ninety-eight percent of the landfalls came to be
On the islands of the Caribbean Sea.

The monopoly was ended in sixteen eighty-eight,
And the import quota ended ten years later,
Because the competition wanted in on the trade,
Especially the Bristol Merchant Venturers.

Negroes were of higher value, being slaves for life.
The import duty was eight times as much per head:
Two shillings and six pence for a European child,
For a Negro, one pound sterling instead.

On the first day of November in sixteen ninety-eight
On a ship called Society of London,
Four hundred twenty-three Negro slaves were imported.
Thomas Ely paid the duties upon them.

This had never happened in Maryland before.
The shipping records show no more than eight on any ship.
Negro children in the Order Books of Chesapeake courts
Were fewer than two hundred, altogether, before this.

We know the racial breakdown for certain.
They were taxable at sixteen years of age,
Which is why the Negro children were examined by the court,
Though each of them would always be a slave.

To be clear, these numbers only count the children
Born in Africa, and not on native ground.
The men and women brought here, and the children who were born here,
Are nowhere in court records to be found.

The slave trade now had changed. It would never be the same.
The demand for white slave children would decline,
And that is why the market was flooded with white children
In sixteen ninety and nine. [123]

XIII.

The first slaves in Virginia came from London,
Vagrant boys and girls forced into labor,
Taken from the city streets, and shipped against their will,
On the rationale of doing them a favor.

A deed of "pious" charity, "redeeming" these "poor souls"
From "the idle life of vagabonds," a life of destitution,
Putting them to "use," in "service to the state,"
Bringing them "to goodness," "from misery and ruin."

Far better to be slaves on the plantations
Than orphans on the streets, or so the logic goes.
I do not accept the basic premise
That anyone should own a human soul.

'Tis in the shire of Devon where this all can be examined,
Where so many parish records have survived,
Where the family charts can oft be reconstructed,
Where we can learn the most about their lives.

Of one hundred eighty-one who came from Devon,
Only four can be identified as orphans.
Twenty-seven lost their father, and six had lost their mother,
Before their date in court across the ocean.

And so, one hundred forty-four were taken
With their father and their mother both alive.
Some of them were poor, but they were not alone.
If allowed to stay at home, they might have thrived.

This was every parent's darkest nightmare,
That a child might without warning disappear.
For some the loss was more than they could bear,
And they died of broken hearts within two years.

Richard Britton, born in Crediton, was taken at age twelve,
Hannah Holland, born in Honiton on Otter,
And Robert Edwards, born in Exeter, were taken at age nine,
And their fathers died of grief for son or daughter.

Some families lost two children, not always both at once.
Sometimes it was one, and then another.
John and William Hogan, born in Landkey, next to Barnstaple,
Were taken three years distant from each other.

Ann and Thomas Butler, born in Exeter,
Taken six years apart, without indentures,
Were transported to Virginia on the very same ship,
The aforesaid Planters Adventure.

Some parents knew their child was captured.
After Ralph Toms, of Plymouth, disappeared,
His father was "subscriber for redemption
Of captives in Turkey and Algiers."

And sure it is no shame, he did not know who to blame
For taking his fourteen year old away.
He might have blamed the gypsies or the faeries,
But the boy was on the Chesapeake Bay.

No child was ever safe from slavery in Devon.
It did not matter if your father was respected.
They took the sons of two parish ministers,
And the son of one parish rector:

William Buckley, David Williams, Thomas Powell.
The family charts have holes within them still.
There was scarcely any voyage to Virginia
Without children taken there against their will. [137]

XIV.

It was sixteen sixty-four in merry England
Where the flowers and the trees can seem like heaven.
In the English Channel, and in the Bristol Channel,
Slave ships sailed along the coasts of Devon.

No child was ever safe from slavery in Devon.
There were three ports of departure for the trade:
Bideford and Plymouth and Topsham.
No child was ever more than thirty miles away.

From all along the southern coast of Devon
And all its estuaries, in the course of forty years,
From at least twenty-six of the parishes,
Someone's son or daughter disappeared.

Little Mathew Ellot was the youngest.
His father died when he was only five.
His mother lost her husband, and then she lost her son,
Never knowing whether Mathew was alive.

He was ordered in Annapolis to serve for thirteen years.
A broken-hearted boy of only seven.
He never more would see the thatched roof on his cottage
In East Budleigh, on the southern coast of Devon.

The northern coast is rugged, and the only estuaries
Are at Bideford on Torridge, and Barnstaple on Taw,
But there could still be danger out on Hartland Point,
From kidnappers, or the constables at law.

Hartland is the place where the coast of Devon turns,
Where the Bristol Channel opens up into the Celtic Sea.
There is a lighthouse on the point, and a harbor in the town,
But the sea cliffs are the special place to be.

The coastal cliffs are carpeted with flowers,
Sea pink and sheeps bit, scurvy grass and heath,
Buttercups and daisies and primroses,
And the slate stands out in ridges on the beach.

From Hartland, John Greenaway was taken,
And brought to Talbot County in Maryland.
From thirteen years of age, he was eight long years a slave,
Never more to see his parents or his Hartland.

The source of Devon's rivers are the peat bogs and the meres
On the barren granite hill tops known as tors,
And the boulder strewn ravines through which rush the streams
That drain the ancient uplands of Dartmoor.

The soils are very thin, and frequent are the winds,
And heavy are the rains that fall from heaven.
The tap roots are not deep, but lovely are the trees,
The stunted, twisted, hawthorn trees of Devon.

Nowhere else in England is there such extent of land
So wild and undisturbed by cultivation,
Bearing on its surface many monuments of stone,
The remains of prehistoric population.

Walkhampton is a village on the west side of Dartmoor,
As remote as almost any place in Devon.
One wonders how, from here, a little boy could disappear.
His name was Robert Atwell, age eleven.

He was twelve years a slave in Virginia.
I would rather die and go to heaven
Than to labor and to wonder if I ever more would see
The stunted, twisted hawthorn trees of Devon,

Or the monuments of stone upon the tor.
There is a folk song that tells about Dartmoor:
"Where every man is equal, for every man is poor.
I would not be where I'm not free as I am upon the moor." [152]

PART TWO

XV.

It may have started out with good intentions.
A servant might arrive without indentures,
If not reduced to writing, or lost while out at sea.
Unless the master and the servant could agree,

There was a need to resolve the matter fairly
As to how many years of service there should be,
And that is why age brackets were established,
By Virginia law, in sixteen forty three.

After Cromwell's invasion of Ireland,
Four hundred Irish children were shipped across the sea
And sold in New England and Virginia
In September of sixteen fifty-three.

And so a law against the Irish was enacted
Lengthening their terms of slavery,
And Virginia made the law retroactive
To September of sixteen fifty-three.

And then, by English law, after sixteen fifty-nine,
Vagrant children could be taken from the streets,
Lawfully by constables, or "spirited" by captains.
The judges never once asked how it happened.

In the year of sixteen sixty, in four counties in Virginia
Where Court Order Books have managed to survive,
There were thirty-three kids without indentures,
And in the two years right before this, only five.

And so the traffic in white children had begun.
Baptismal records show where eight were from:
Newcastle, Edinburgh, Gloucester, and London,
To serve until the age of twenty-one.

But the planters were not satisfied with this.
So Virginia law was modified once more:
If sixteen years of age, you would be five years a slave,
If younger, you would serve till twenty-four.

In Maryland, the sentence would be four to seven years,
Depending on your age when you appeared,
If you came without indentures, quite against your will,
To the blessèd shining city on the hill.

At least five thousand children in the course of sixty years
Were subject to the laws that I have mentioned.
Though this was not the reason why the laws, at first, were written,
The road to hell is paved with good intentions.

Lest anyone suppose that I exaggerate the case
Or resent that I have dared to raise the specter,
Consider the occasions when a kidnapping charge
Is fully supported by the record. [163]

XVI.

His name was John Lime, and he was baptized
A poor boy from Stepney, in London.
And this is the story he told to the court
When he summoned the strength to confront them.

He was spirited out of his own native country,
Unknown to his family and friends,
And shipped as a servant to Somerset County
From one of the ports on the Thames.

He was judged to be fifteen to eighteen years old,
And ordered to serve seven years.
He said he'd been given some sort of indentures
Which, on board the ship, disappeared.

To the court in Charles County came seven young men
With indentures for terms of four years.
They had all served their time, and petitioned for freedom,
And Captain John Bowman appeared.

He swore under oath he remembered the seven,
Had read their indentures on board of his ship,
And he still possessed all the counterpart copies
Sufficient to prove all of this.

The Captain pronounced them "kidnappers indentures."
Those are the words on the record.
And as to the motive to keep these men captive,
There is no need for conjecture.

Five of the seven were owned by two judges
Who had an ulterior purpose:
To rule the indentures invalid, and send
The petitioners back to their service.

Think what this means. If the men had agreed
To come in the first place, they would have been freed.
Because they were kidnapped, the papers weren't real.
They were punished for lack of a notary seal.

The ship, said John Bowman, had sailed from Gravesend,
The main port of London, downstream on the Thames.
And we know it arrived at the very same time
As the poor boy from London, John Lime.

It brought them to two different Maryland counties
On opposite shores of the Chesapeake Bay,
And in two different courts we hear the same story,
When neither one knew what the other would say. [173]

XVII.

Rather than stand in the rain,
I wandered into the library,
And a woman began to explain
What she knew of her own ancestry.

"We have a legend in our family
From seventeenth century New England
About a boy who was lured aboard a ship
And they sailed away with him.

His father was from Scotland,
The family name was Waughop."
So I showed her in my book
A boy named Thomas Walcupp.

In the year sixteen ninety-eight,
In Northumberland County, Virginia,
He was ordered at nine years of age
To be fifteen years a slave.

So I pulled up the record of his birth
And we began to peruse it:
Born in sixteen eighty-nine
In Framingham, Massachusetts.

His father's name was George.
Naomi was his mother.
She told me this was the boy.
He was her ancestor's brother.

Whenever a child disappears,
The family remembers the story.
It is simply not the same
As when a child is buried.

And now, three centuries on,
A man seeking shelter from the rain
Solves the age old mystery
That the family never could explain. [181]

XVIII.

When children were sentenced to slavery,
Their master had no obligations.
They were not as lucky as orphans
With enforceable court stipulations.

Orphans were all to have washing and lodging,
And clothing both woolen and linen,
And be taught how to read from the Bible
In the lawful established religion.

Some orphans were sent to a school
For six months or a year, maybe two,
And taught how to write in a legible hand,
Which many, back then, could not do.

Sometimes the boys were apprenticed
To a tanner, a joiner, a cooper, a tailor,
A blacksmith, a shipwright, a carpenter,
A shoemaker, or a cordwainer.

All were to have at the end of their terms
A suit of apparel quite decent:
Hat and shoes and stockings and shirt
And coat and jacket and breeches.

Some were given a fine set of tools,
Or a cow with a calf by her side,
Or a horse and a bridle and saddle
For the young man to mount and to ride.

But the servants imported from elsewhere,
By law, were not deemed to deserve this.
Whether or not with indentures,
They were allowed at the end of their service:

In Maryland, one suit of clothes,
And also one axe and two hoes,
And three barrels of Indian corn,
With no land to plant it upon.

In Virginia, ten bushels of corn,
Thirty shillings and one well fixed musket,
And likewise no land of their own.
But in a twist of colonial justice,

Those who transported the settlers,
Whether freemen or servants or children,
Were rewarded with generous land grants
Of fifty acres per person. [191]

XIX.

John Ward was an orphan boy in sixteen fifty-two.
He came into the country at the age of four or five.
And now, at nine or ten, he agreed to an indenture,
And he made his mark upon it, to survive.

In return for meat and drink, and lodging and apparel,
He would serve his master, Arthur Turner,
Who would teach the boy to read, or hire a tutor,
Or teach him the trade of a carpenter or cooper.

And at the age of twenty, when his term of service ended,
Arthur Turner was to grant him fifty acres,
A cow, and a sow, and his freedom corn and clothing.
Two witnesses had signed the piece of paper.

It was sixteen sixty-three when the Charles County Court
Summoned Arthur Turner to explain
Why the orphan boy was "so ill treated in his house
That the voice of the people cryeth shame."

He was found in "a most rotten filthy stinking lodge,"
His clothes were "all ragged and torn,"
His hair was all dusty "with ashes,"
And the Court set him free as he was born.

John Ward faced the world with next to nothing.
But he was lucky that they even let him loose.
It was the first time in Charles County history
That a servant had been freed due to abuse. [197]

XX.

When children were brought to the Chesapeake Bay
They were more or less trapped, and could not run away.
Not knowing the lay of the land they were in,
With no one to guide them, their chances were slim.

They were all on peninsulas, in between rivers
Where ships could sail inland at least thirty miles,
They must bypass the wagon roads all in between,
Where runaway children were easily seen.

The Coastal Plain reaches inland to the falls
Where the rivers descend from the foothills,
And this was the limit of travel by boat.
Beyond this the homesteads were few and remote.

A horse trail developed on top of the cliffs,
On the Fall Line, connecting one fall to another,
But runaways crossing by ferry or bridge
Were in danger of being discovered.

The forts of the frontier were located here,
And a wagon road built in sixteen ninety-one,
Where many a runaway servant was caught
And returned to the master from whom he had run.

So they had to keep traveling, into the wilderness,
Somewhere beyond the long arm of the law,
Beyond the encroachments of settlers,
To lands the white man seldom saw. [203]

XXI.

"Runaway time" is what they called it,
When a servant was absent from his master.
In Virginia the punishment was mild,
In Maryland, an absolute disaster.

In Virginia, it was two days of servitude
For each day of runaway time.
In Maryland, ten days for every one day.
The words were emphasized and underlined.

And the judges could tack on months, or even years,
For the cost of "taking up" a servant.
If you ran far away, or were gone a long time,
Or your capture involved many persons,

The numbers very quickly added up.
A punitive example, not to be outdone,
Was twenty months servitude for six days absence,
More than one hundred to one.

Each person "taking up" a suspect
Earned two hundred pounds of tobacco,
To be paid by the owner of the runaway slave,
But the law applied to travelers also.

Anyone "not sufficiently known,
Or able to give a good account of himself,"
Even if a free man, taken by mistake,
Had to pay the fine to his captors, or else

The Court could sentence him to slavery,
Which did happen twice in Charles County.
James Fuller was taken by Sheriff John Bayne,
But luckily, he could pay the bounty.

Taken into custody by Sheriff Walter Story
Was an innocent man, John Lee,
Who was sentenced to two years of slavery.
They called it "satisfaction for his fees."

And this is why the right to travel freely,
At the birth of the American nation,
Was the very first right of the people
In the Articles of Confederation. [212]

XXII.

Negroes, if they ran away, were never brought to Court.
They were slaves for life, so there wasn't any point.
They could not be sentenced to any extra time.
They were punished by their masters for their crime.

They could be whipped, or even beaten, with impunity.
It was not a crime if they should happen to be killed,
For no man, by intention, would destroy his own estate.
It was therefore without malice, not at will.

Mulattos were enslaved until the age of thirty-one,
Except adopted orphans with approval from the Court:
Orphan girls, by law, were free at sixteen years of age,
Orphan boys upon the age of twenty-one.

Mulattos, if they ran away, were treated without mercy.
Sometimes the master waited till the slave was thirty-one,
And upon the verge of freedom he would bring him back to Court,
And have him punished then for what he long ago had done.

John Glover, a Mulatto, nine months over thirty-one,
Was sentenced to nine hundred twenty days.
Thomas Fountain, a Mulatto, two months shy of thirty-one,
Got one hundred months for having run away.

A man known as "Mollatto Will" was sentenced to nine years.
He would not be free until the age of forty,
The second longest sentence from the Charles County Court,
But there were indentured servants with such stories. [218]

XXIII.

Rosamond Law was absent twice.
We know nothing more about her.
First one master, then another
Did not want to be without her.

The first time she was captured
She got four years from the Court,
And when nine years had passed and gone
They gave her nine years more.

We don't know what happened then.
Perhaps she served for eighteen years,
Or maybe ran away again,
And this time disappeared.

Silent Ball was gone five times
In less than seven years.
The Court was without mercy
Every time she reappeared.

They gave her ten days servitude
For every one day's absence,
As incentive to run off again
At each one of her chances.

Seven years she owed to three
Exasperated masters.
They gave up on her only when
She gave birth to a bastard.

John Bacon was a servant
To a "Worshipful Commissioner"
Who sat as a presiding judge
When he was the petitioner.

For almost eight months absence
John Bacon got ten days to one,
Plus five hundred extra days
Because the math was wrong.

I don't know who did the math,
Or which judge was the villain,
But Henry Hawkins owned already
Fourteen kidnapped children. [227]

XXIV.

There was a young servant in Maryland.
Her name was Elizabeth Hasellton.
It appears that she did have indentures.
Her master was Nicholas Emanson.

She was absent three times from her master
For thirty-eight days altogether,
And her mistress did take it upon herself,
In place of the Court, to correct her.

When she served her six years of indenture,
And the date of her freedom was nearing,
Her master demanded more punishment,
And brought her to Court for a hearing.

But to the surprise of her master,
She actually had an attorney.
She refused to provide satisfaction,
And the Sheriff impaneled a jury.

Richard and Lewis, the sons of the mistress,
Both testified that their mother did beat her,
Put her in irons, took her to Virginia,
And said after that she would free her.

Edmond Lambert once captured the servant,
And carried her home to her mistress,
He said she was tied to a bed post,
And he said that the mistress had whipped her.

But it was Anne Lane, who was once at the house,
And afterwards entered to sweep with a broom,
Who said that she witnessed "great wounds in her back,"
And "a puddle of blood in the room."

Anne Lane was herself a survivor,
Kidnapped and sold as a servant.
She was free after five years of slavery,
And now she was keenly observant.

The jury acquitted Elizabeth Hasellton.
Nicholas Emanson paid all her costs.
If she had not retained an attorney,
Her case likely would have been lost.

This occurred in the year sixteen seventy,
And this was the first time in history
That the Charles County Court would implicitly say
There were reasons for running away. [237]

XXV.

Abigail Clampett, indentured servant,
Was brought to Court for running away.
Confessing only ten days absence,
She would serve one hundred days.

Her day in Court was not yet done.
From her former master she had run.
Cornelius Maddock was his name.
He had come to Court "to prove ye same."

Abigail Clampett, in open Court,
In the presence of Cornelius Maddock,
Stripped herself "from ye waist upwards,"
Exposing "to ye Justices"

On "Back and Belly, Arms and Wrists
Many marks" upon her person,
"Severe and cruel whippings and tyings
Whilst she was Maddock's servant."

The Court acquitted Abigail Clampett
Of any debt to Cornelius Maddock.
Her courage was a sight to see
In seventeen o three. [242]

XXVI.

His name was John Green, and his age was fourteen.
He came in the year of sixteen sixty eight.
He was ordered to serve for eight years as a slave,
Up the Potomac from Chesapeake Bay.

Benjamin Rozer, the High Sheriff, sold him
To one Daniell Johnson, a wealthy young man,
A planter with two thousand acres of land
All signed and sealed by the governor's hand.

In less than three years Daniell Johnson had died,
And one Francis Kilbourne, who married his bride,
Carried John Green above Piscataway,
Far from the shores of the Chesapeake Bay.

He was there left alone on a frontier plantation
To fend for himself at the risk of starvation
Without enough clothing, and no neighbors near him,
A frightened young lad at the mercy of Indians.

And so he contracted with one Philip Lynes
To work the north side of Piscataway River,
Extending his service for two years more time
Than the sentence the Charles County Court had delivered.

No servant, by law, whether sentenced or hired,
Could agree to more years till the first term expired,
For any such bargain is under duress,
And so the agreement was of no effect.

And when his original eight years were done,
He traveled, somehow, fifteen miles to the town,
He petitioned for freedom, the Court set him free,
As according to law he had full right to be.

We do not know what became of him then.
He never appears on the record again.
But though he is shrouded in mystery,
He is a pivotal figure in history.

Of all the successful petitions for freedom,
This is the one to remember,
For this was the first one that ever had come
From a servant who had no indentures. [251]

XXVII.

Philip Lynes, born in Holborn, in the very heart of London,
Came to Charles County and became a wealthy man.
He had more than fifty servants, and seven thousand acres,
Beginning at Piscataway, where first he purchased land.

He was sworn as an attorney at the age of twenty-nine,
And he learned how to manipulate the system.
More than thirty masters were complained of by petitions,
But only one repeatedly had victims.

In March of sixteen eighty, a man named Thomas Smith,
A hired hand to Philip Lynes, was on his way to Court,
To testify in person, in front of a Grand Jury.
And Philip intercepted him in fury.

He beat him with his cane until it broke,
But the Court refused to punish or to fine him,
Because he did it out of ignorance, not knowing
The reason why his hired hand was going.

After that, all manner of neglect, abuse, and beatings
Were left unto the many overseers of Philip Lynes.
The victims often named them in the County Court proceedings,
But not a single one of them was punished for his crimes.

Henry Goodrick, Overseer, was forbidden, "at his peril,"
To abuse or give "correction" to John Lew.
Henry Shalter, a Petitioner, was taken from John Bould
In whose hands he was much "beaten and abused."

Catherine Jones, abused by Henry Thompson, Overseer,
Was removed from the plantation where she'd been,
And Henry Thompson once had been a child without indentures.
He was doing unto others what had once been done to him.

Indicted and arrested was a man named James Lewis,
For killing Philip's servant, Owen Carr.
He was released from County jail for being cold and without clothes.
It was ironic for the County Court to do this,

For his servant Adam Wharton, "found in Captain Warren's quarter,
Naked of all clothes and in a perishing condition,"
Was ordered by the Court to be returned to Philip Lynes,
Who reimbursed the Captain, but he never paid a fine.

A servant named Teague Turlayes oftentimes did run away,
In all, two hundred forty days. His sentence was two thousand days.
The Court reduced his sentence, for he came so many times
To complain about his treatment at the hands of Philip Lines.

This was in November. He was made to spend the winter
Without clothing, without lodging, and not "a bed to lie on."
Three times more he came to Court to let the judges know.
But nothing ever happened because Philip did not show.

It was also in November when three servants came to Court,
James Thornborough, Edward Darnell, Catherine Jones.
They were naked and "were almost starved." So the record shows.
To keep them all "from perishing," the Court provided clothes.

One year later, in November, Catherine Jones was back in Court,
"A poor distressed and almost naked servant."
"Under several Overseers" she was "kept so bare of clothes
That she was almost perished" from the cold,

"Constantly compelled to do her labor almost naked."
A shift and linen petticoat were all she had to wear.
She asked the Court for discharge or for lenience,
Knowing Philip Lynes "gives no manner of obedience."

He was ordered to provide his servant with "good woolen clothes,"
And also "shoes and stockings" for "to keep her from the cold."
We don't know if she survived, for she does not turn up again
As petitioner for freedom from Philip and his men. [266]

XXVIII.

There were many servants who had fully served their time,
And still their masters would not let them go.
So they had to go to Court, to petition for their freedom,
And also for their "freedom corn and clothes."

Children coming in without indentures
Were safer in this one and only way:
Their servitude was based upon an order from the Court,
And they could expect their freedom on a stipulated day.

Most of the petitioners were servants with indentures,
And their masters tried to get a Court decision
That the document was "void," or not "good and authentic,"
Or "in need of further proof," or "not sufficient."

Nearly every master, if he failed in this attempt,
Never more would challenge an indenture.
But the aforesaid Philip Lynes did try and fail nine times –
The one and only multiple offender.

Two produced indentures, registered and sealed,
The truth of which the judges knew for certain.
Two provided statements from the shippers,
One by affidavit, one in person.

Three were backed by those who made the sale to Philip Lynes,
Or witnesses who saw the sale, and knew for how much time.
One procured a witness from Anne Arundel County,
And the Court provided one with an attorney.

And there can be no question of his purpose:
To extract from them more months or years of service.
Each one of the nine was forced to serve more time,
And only one got compensation from his master, Philip Lynes.

The monster Philip Lynes died in seventeen o nine.
And he left as the first item in his Will,
To purchase "mourning rings," ten pounds sterling each,
To his connections in the city on the hill:

To Madam Jean Seymour, third wife of the Governor,
To Mrs. Mary Contee, favorite cousin of the Governor,
To Captain Thomas Seymour, the brother of the Governor,
And Mr. William Bladen, a Royal Naval Officer,

Who collected import duties on the "cargo,"
The rum, and the tobacco, and the "servants."
Think of all the children so abused by Philip Lines,
And their master well connected to the serpents. [276]

XXIX.

Henry Hardy was a bastard child from Burnley, Lancashire,
Stigmatized at birth, in parish records, without mercy.
At eighteen years of age he was shipped to Charles County.
A lad without indentures, he was sold to Thomas Percy.

He became a free man at the age of twenty-four,
Was sworn as an Attorney at the age of forty-five,
And at the age of fifty was appointed and ordained
A "Worshipful Commissioner," such a pious name.

He was doing unto others what had once been done to him,
He could sentence kids to service almost monthly,
"According to the law," or as they liked to say in Maryland:
"According to the custom of the country."

Anne Ashman was a widow when she married Henry Hardy.
She had six children, all four boys were minors.
Less than four years later, in need of arbitration,
And divorce not being legal, she sued for separation.

She still had ninety acres at the head of Baker Creek.
She wanted for to live there with her children.
But with Henry on the bench, the proceeding was a mockery.
The husband claimed the children as his property.

Seventeen months later she returned with a complaint
Of her husband's harsh, ill usage of her children,
That they might be taken from him, and all bound out to trades.
But they were made to sign indentures for to serve him.

After Henry Hardy had retired from the bench,
His wife complained of his harsh usage of her,
She said she could not live with him, and Henry did consent,
But the boys would not be living with their mother.

And then a deposition was entered on the record.
Mary Symmons, one of Henry Hardy's servants,
Nineteen years of age, had sworn before a justice
That he often forced himself upon her person,

She said he tried to rape her, and made a threat to kill her
"If she did not yield to his lustful desires,
And often used most filthy ways by taking out his nakedness"
To force it "in her hand and otherwise."

Whereupon "your Worships" did deliberate the matter.
Henry Hardy was acquitted and discharged.
The Court moved on to other matters. They enslaved another woman,
With the monster Henry Hardy still at large.

And sure it was no wonder, Mary Symmons ran away.
Henry caught her and he brought her into Court without delay,
Expecting they would punish her. The Court did not agree.
Much to his surprise, they set her free.

This happened long ago, in seventeen o six,
But in some ways nothing much has really changed.
The authorities might not believe the victim,
Even when the perpetrator is deranged. [288]

XXX.

This is the story of Captain John Bayne
And his penchant for twelve year old boys,
How he used his positions of power,
These innocent lives to destroy.

In two different Maryland counties
He inherited land from his father,
Who died when John Bayne was a boy,
And the children were raised by their mother.

When John was a young man he bought his first boy,
And he had not come here on purpose.
He was fourteen years old, but he looked to be twelve,
And was forced into ten years of service.

When eight years had passed, he would soon need another.
He bought himself two fresh new faces,
One for himself, and one for his mother.
He now had a boy in both places.

And then he obtained from the Charles County Court
A license to be an innkeeper.
He could serve meals at a fixed time and price,
But he was not allowed to serve liquor.

He could provide lodging for travelers,
And stables to shelter their horses,
But was not to allow "any evil,"
In which case his license was forfeit.

A scant nine months later John Bayne was indicted
For selling strong liquor on Sunday.
He pleaded not guilty, a jury was called,
He was tried and acquitted in one day.

Eighteen months later it happened again.
He was faced with a six count indictment
For selling hard liquor and cider and wine,
And this time without any license.

This time the witnesses numbered fourteen.
Among those who lined up against him
Were two of the judges who sat on the Court,
And survivors who had no indentures.

But there was no trial. His case was appealed
To a court room in St. Mary's County,
Where John Bayne just happened to sit on a court,
And he used his influence profoundly.

Six months after that he bought two Irish lads.
He brought them to St. Mary's County,
Where he could pass sentence upon them himself,
While staying quite clear of Charles County,

Until, on June ninth of sixteen ninety six,
When he came with a Royal Commission
Appointing him Charles County Sheriff,
And there could be no opposition.

He hand-picked his deputy, one Thomas Whichaley.
Now he could act with impunity.
And he began purchasing twelve year old boys
For his inn, at his first opportunity.

John Bryan, John Rye, Alex Mills,
John Magrah and Anthony Coney,
All were adjudged to be twelve years of age
When examined like so many ponies.

All of them now would be owned for ten years
By the Sheriff who called himself "Captain."
He could do what he wanted, with no one to hear
Or look into whatever might happen.

He bought three teenagers, all captured in Scotland,
To work in the fields with the two Irish lads.
The last boy he purchased was eight years of age,
The youngest John Bayne ever had.

After John Bayne had served two terms as Sheriff,
He sat as a justice at Charles County Court.
He attended three sessions in seventeen hundred,
And then his career was cut short.

On October the fifth he dictated his will,
Which witnesses later all swore that he signed,
Though when it was closely examined in Court
It was found to be "blotted" and much "interlined."

The Captain would not write it over,
Having hitherto readied his horses,
To carry him down to the docks
At the port island known as Saint Georges.

Seven weeks later, his mother
Expressed her concern with her pen:
He might not "return safe out of England."
They never heard from him again. [308]

XXXI.

The Captain is missing, oh where can he be?
He left in a coach, and two horses had he,
For to go fifty miles to the docks on the sea.
The Captain is missing, oh where can he be?

The Captain is missing, oh where did he go?
He could have been ambushed, and no one would know,
With many deep waters alongside his way,
Drowned in a river, or drowned in a bay.

The Captain is missing, did he make the trip?
Did he get to Saint Georges and sail on the ship?
Did he arrive safely, or drown in the sea?
The Captain is missing, oh where can he be?

Did he make it to Liverpool, where he was going?
By far the most difficult part is not knowing.
Month after month there is nary a word.
Oh where is the Captain, why have we not heard?

They never would find him, for they could not search
In the burial ground of Saint Nicholas Church.
He landed in Liverpool, died four months later,
'Tis all written down in the Archbishop's papers.

"John Bayne of Virginia," the death record said,
So no one in Maryland knew he was dead.
The Captain went missing, as had the child slaves
That he owned and abused till he went to his grave. [314]

XXXII.

The Captain's estate was now out of control.
Unless his dead body washed up on the shoals,
His wife, the Executrix, could not take charge,
For no one could prove he was not still at large.

The Captain was missing for more than a year
When Colonel John Courts felt compelled to appear
On behalf of his God Son, a boy named John Warren,
A fatherless, motherless, derelict orphan

Left in the care of the Captain John Bayne,
Who had leased the boy's land unto one William Hawton,
And he, with five servants, had cut all the trees
Destroying the land of which they were trustees.

And the boy, in the keeping of Madam Anne Bayne,
Was "brought up to idleness, swearing and vices."
His God Father promised to plant him an orchard,
And teach him to read and write. It was so ordered.

In a year and a half the estate was obtained
By "insinuation" of Madam Anne Bayne.
Based upon whatever words she had said,
The County Court ruled that the Captain was dead.

To his children, named Ebsworth and Walter and Anne,
He left more than three thousand acres of land.
Twelve Negroes and all of the servants were owned
By his wife, till the children were married or grown.

The Scots-Irish field hands, all five had escaped,
The ones made to ravage the orphan's estate.
But the boys of the brothel, all five did remain
The private possessions of Madam Anne Bayne.

There were ten other servants all mentioned by name.
Some had indentures, and others were orphans.
They appeared on the list between Negroes and cows,
Or else with the bulls and the horses.

Walter, in time, ended up with the boys.
John Bryan, the last of the five to gain freedom,
Was rescued by one of the Irish field hands
Who swore to what went on "between" them.

John Bryan had lost both his parents at sea
And was raised by a kind, wealthy captain,
Or so goes the legend his family now tells,
But that is not quite how it happened. [324]

PART THREE

XXXIII.

The "Germantown Protest" of sixteen eighty eight,
Drafted by the Mennonites and Quakers,
Was the first written protest against slavery,
With words to this effect upon the paper:

Are there any who would want to be handled in this manner?
How fearful and faint hearted are many on the sea
When they see a strange vessel, and know they might be taken
And sold into slavery in Turkey.

It is worse for those who say they are Christians
To bring them hitherto without consent,
No matter whether purchased or stolen,
Or what their age, or color, or descent.

And though they are black, we cannot conceive
There is any more liberty to have them as slaves
Than there is for to have other white ones
And to hold them in bondage till the grave.

This was written at the home of Richard Worrel,
And there were only four brave men who signed it.
There was not a schism or a quarrel,
But no one else, in writing, stood behind it. [329]

XXXIV.

The Pennsylvania Charter was granted by the King
On the fourth of March in sixteen eighty one.
It is said that by the end of the very next year
Two thousand settlers had come.

The first white slave ship on the record
Arrived at Philadelphia in sixteen eighty two,
The Antelope of Belfast, Edward Cooke the Master.
The passengers named are only two.

42

But this is the same ship, the Antelope of Belfast,
That carried a child named Proo Matharoon
Up the James River to York County, Virginia.
One child without indentures equals proof.

The Concord of London, William Jefferies the Commander,
Arrived at Philadelphia in sixteen eighty-three.
Five hundred tons, with thirty-two guns,
In the service of the British Royal Navy.

It was under the command of Thomas Grantham
When it sailed five times to James River,
Headed for York County with its cargo
Of twenty-one children to deliver.

And this was the same William Jefferies
Who sailed the Golden Fortune twice before,
And later the Sarah, with at least nine children,
To the counties of Middlesex and York.

The Jeffries of London, Thomas Arnold the Commander,
Arrived at Philadelphia in sixteen eighty-six.
And a child, John Le Marr, came to Middlesex County.
Thomas Arnold brought him on the very same ship.

And this was the same Thomas Arnold
Who imported two kids on the Richard and Jane,
And fifteen kids on the Henry and Anne.
To York and to Middlesex counties they came.

He took them not only from London,
But from Scotland and Devon and Cheshire.
We may as well call him what he was:
A pirate absconding with his treasure. [338]

XXXV.

The Elizabeth and Mary, in sixteen eighty-three,
And the Margaret of London, in sixteen eighty-seven,
Arrived at Philadelphia with "servants" for the planters,
And John Bowman was the master or commander.

John Bowman had a history. Back in sixteen seventy
The Pelican of London first appears upon the record
When two children at York County did identify the ship,
But these were not his only victims ever.

Buried on the web where it is very hard to find
Is a database of London shipping records.
John Bowman, for a decade, was the master of the ship,
And he sailed it to Virginia on at least six trips.

And then he made three trips on the Elizabeth and Mary,
Just one of many masters who had brought her out to sea.
Kids without indentures did identify this ship
From sixteen fifty eight until seventeen o three.

His trip upon the Margaret was in sixteen eighty-seven.
And the ship made five more voyages to Maryland,
The last in sixteen ninety-eight, with import duties paid
On forty-three white "servants." They did not call them slaves.

This is the same John Bowman who, in June of sixteen ninety,
Appeared in Charles County Court in Maryland,
And stated that he knowingly transported kidnap victims,
And the judges were protective of the system.

This is the last time we find John Bowman on the record.
This may have been the close of his career,
At least twelve trips, upon at least three ships,
Covering the space of twenty years.

There is a place called Bowman's Hill in Bucks County, Pennsylvania.
As to how it got its name, there is a legend
About a pirate named John Bowman who is buried on the hill,
As near as he would ever get to heaven. [346]

XXXVI.

When John Bowman referred to "kidnappers indentures,"
Quite unashamed of his wording so flagrant,
All that they lacked was a notary seal.
The papers in question were signed by an agent.

His name was John Williams, a merchant in London.
John Bowman was captain on this very trip.
He said he "transported them into this country"
And read their indentures "aboard of his ship."

In sixteen eighty-five the young victims arrived.
The following winter the seven were sentenced.
The records of London tell more of the tale,
Suggesting the ship on which Bowman set sail.

John Williams, the merchant, was also a mariner,
Out on the sea in sixteen eighty-five
In a ship called Elizabeth, he was the master,
And remained so at least five years after.

In sixteen eighty-three, on the sixth of December,
We find on the record a brutal indenture.
A child of sixteen was to serve for nine years,
And the name of the agent, John Williams, appears.

Of eighty-two filed in this box of indentures,
Only sixteen are for more than four years.
The one for nine years was the longest of all.
'Twas better to have no indentures at all.

The child was conveyed on a ship called the Judith.
The name of the captain was one Mathew Trim.
In sixteen eighty-four, at York County, Virginia,
One of the children identified him.

In sixteen eighty-five he was not the commander.
A search of the name of the same Mathew Trim
Finds him in August, in London, at Court.
An indictment had named an accomplice and him.

He had assaulted Elizabeth Partridge,
Conveyed her aboard of his ship called the Indy,
Brought her somewhere in Virginia and sold her.
Nineteen such cases are found in this folder.

His indictment was dated sixteen eighty-two.
It appears he was never convicted of this.
He brought a slave child "in the good Shippe ye Indy,"
York County, Virginia, sixteen eighty-six.

He later commanded the Judith again,
And sailed in a convoy en route to the Thames,
With the Concord and Jeffreys, two of the ships
At the Delaware River, on previous trips.

The records of London show thirty indictments,
Sometimes with multiple kidnapping victims.
More often than not we do not know the outcome,
But some of them did go to prison.

Consider the wording of this,
An indictment of one of the women:
"For selling her servant Ann Parker
To be a slave in Virginia."

The issue was not the kidnapping itself.
The constables captured whoever they saw.
But only the good guys could do this.
It all had to happen according to law. [360]

XXXVII.

Kidnapped children, when they came without indentures,
Would be sentenced at the Court of Quarter Sessions.
And if servants ran away and then were seized
They would be sentenced at the Court of Common Pleas.

In Philadelphia these records have been lost,
Though all the deeds and wills have yet survived.
The oldest Quarter Sessions are from seventeen nineteen,
Except for part of sixteen ninety five,

And those fragments end on the first week of September,
Just days before a white slave ship arrived.
Kids without indentures came to Chester County Court
On October first of sixteen ninety five.

This was not the first time at Chester County Court.
Eight boys without indentures came in sixteen ninety-three,
Brought into this country by a man named Maurice Trent.
The youngest were eleven, the oldest were fourteen.

Six boys without indentures came in sixteen ninety-five,
All of them brought in by Maurice Trent.
They were brought to Court the first day of October.
Soon afterward his smuggling days were over.

His brigantine was seized off the west coast of New Jersey,
For smuggling tobacco, not having paid the tax,
And sailing with his cargo directly into Scotland,
Contrary to the Navigation Acts.

In the summer and the fall of sixteen ninety-seven
The courts were overwhelmed by kids without indentures.
Most or all of them arrived in the third week of July,
Still crowding the court docket in December.

There were fifty-five in all at Chester County,
Eight more at Bucks and Burlington and Kent,
And those who named the seller on the record
Said they bought the children from James Trent.

But his slave trading days would soon be over.
His will was proved in sixteen ninety-eight.
To his brother, William Trent, of Philadelphia,
His Executor, he left his whole estate.

Maurice Trent, and James Trent, and William Trent.
The whole thing was a family operation.
Fourteen more kids appeared, all in the next three years,
While the slave trade found another prime location. [370]

XXXVIII.

The brothers Trent, from Inverness, in Scotland,
Came to Pennsylvania when the colony was chartered
In sixteen eighty-one, and right away they started
Selling children, leaving families broken hearted.

Their uncle was a merchant in Edinburgh, Scotland.
The ships sailed mainly from the Port of Leith,
Taking children even from the offshore islands,
The Shetlands, the Orkneys, and the Hebrides,

From the streets of London and Dublin,
From Northumberland, Inverness, and Perth,
From the shires of Cheshire and Devon,
To sell for whatever they were worth.

Maurice Trent died in sixteen ninety-seven,
James Trent died in sixteen ninety-eight.
William Trent was the sole surviving brother.
And he amassed a fabulous estate.

He was perhaps the richest man in Philadelphia.
He would buy and sell whatever he could trade:
Wine and rum and flour and furs,
Molasses and tobacco and slaves.

He owned, in part, more than forty sailing ships,
And some of these were carrying white slaves,
As we know from the records of the Chesapeake courts,
Or from the import duties that they paid.

The Sarah, the Mary, the Globe of London,
The Diligence of London, the Dove, the Jane,
The Happy Union, the Susannah,
And the Richard and Sarah, by name.

We don't know who was sold in Philadelphia.
We don't have any of their names.
We don't know what happened to the records.
The rumor is they all went up in flames.

But it seems, from the names in the Chesapeake courts,
Pennsylvania, for a time, was the center of the trade,
For the numbers decline in sixteen eighty-one,
And rise again in sixteen ninety-eight. [379]

XXXIX.

Having said all this, I must admit
That children brought to Chester County
Faced a future not so bleak
As those brought to the Chesapeake.

The boys were all so very young.
Their average age was thirteen years.
The girls were somewhat older.
And who would dry their tears?

Of sixty-six who bought these kids,
Fifty-three, at least, were Quakers.
Servants, when their time expired,
By law were promised fifty acres.

Most were taught to read and write.
Some were taught a trade.
But these were kidnapped children,
And some were still afraid.

One did try to kill himself,
And tried to run away.
All he got was eight months time
And warning to behave.

One did steal a gelding bay
And got away on horseback.
He was fined, and got more time,
And lashes on his bare back.

Thirteen kids have marriage records.
Three of these were set free early.
None were kept beyond their time.
None said they were treated poorly.

Thirteen are found as grown adults
Owning land in Chester County,
Though none of them were issued deeds
Till seventeen and thirty three.

Sixty of the children
Who arrived without indentures
Cannot be found as grown adults
In Chester County records.

The reason why is crystal clear.
They did not simply disappear.
'Twas Scots and Irish pioneers
Who settled the frontier.

The Quakers and the Mennonites
Were pacifists who would not fight.
All they wanted was to farm
And raise their children safe from harm.

They settled on the farmland
That would yield the biggest bounty,
All upon the coastal plain
Of Lancaster and Chester Counties.

The Scots and Irish were content
To farm for their subsistence
In the Appalachian Mountains
As the first line of resistance

To the Indians upon whose lands
They were, in fact, encroaching.
They were hunting for survival.
They would not have thought it poaching.

A cabin in the wilderness,
A little family garden,
Distant from the government.
To them it seemed a bargain. [394]

XL.

In seventeen thirty, when Lancaster County
Was newly carved out of the County of Chester,
Adventurous men of Scots-Irish descent
Fearlessly migrated westward.

As many as forty had been stolen children,
Sold off as slaves at the Delaware River,
Promised free land when their service was over,
But no deeds had yet been delivered.

Many Scots-Irish had lived on "The Manor,"
Upon the east bank of the wild Susquehanna,
But having no title to lands on these waters,
The constables viewed them as squatters.

The land agent wanted to gather them all
In a Scots-Irish township they called Donegal.
The "militant settlers" were directed here,
Between pacifist Mennonites and the frontier.

But the freemen were not of a mind to withdraw.
They claimed fifty acres as promised by law.
They could not pay for it, and all stood their ground,
So the land agent ordered their cabins torn down.

These were resilient young women and men.
They rebuilt their settlements, time and again.
They knew the land agent would certainly fail,
So remote from the courts and without any jail.

When the colony set up a county around them,
The arm of the law had decisively found them.
Twenty-nine homes were destroyed, every one.
And James Logan bragged about what he had done.

He called them all "vagabonds," "dissolute people,"
Squatters among the "legitimate settlers."
In middle of winter he left them all there
With the panthers, the wolves, and the bears.

The survivors set out on an Indian trail,
Loaded with all they could carry,
To a trading post set up at Harrisburg,
Where the waters were easily ferried.

The trail entered into the Cumberland Valley,
Eighty miles long and eleven miles wide,
Farmland as fertile as anywhere found,
Bounded by mountains along either side.

To the southeast the mountains were easily bypassed
Where rivers flowed through, in between them.
To the northwest the mountains seemed endless,
And very few white men had seen them.

This was the land called the "Valley and Ridge,"
With parallel mountains of primeval forest,
Where backwoodsmen had to cut paths for themselves,
In search of the routes that were shortest.

Sometimes the rivers that flowed down the slopes
Had at their headwaters excellent passes.
But each mountain ridge required more exploration.
Each one inhibited westward migration.

Each mountain pass took some time to discover.
They never lined up from one ridge to another.
And when at long last the explorers had seen them,
They had to traverse the long valleys between them.

Sometimes the rivers would cut through them all,
For the rivers are older than all of the ridges.
As mountains were ever so slowly uplifted,
The valleys of rivers were deepened, not shifted.

From the wild Susquehanna unto the Potomac,
From one water gap to the other,
The Scots and the Irish were right in the middle.
The mountains would serve as a buffer.

Here was a place they could truly be free,
In the middle of nowhere, at Middle Spring Creek.
They built their own town, and they built their own church,
They made their own laws, and they farmed their own dirt.

The history books tell us that Scots-Irish settlers
Came to this valley in seventeen thirty,
The very same year they were chased from "The Manor,"
The opposite shore of the wild Susquehanna.

It was twenty more years before Cumberland County
Intruded upon what was then the wild west.
Deeds were delivered, and taxes collected.
Courts were established, and records were kept.

Of sixty-six surnames of former child slaves
Not found as free men near the County of Chester,
Two-thirds, forty-four, can be located here
As owners of land, or in the court records.

'Tis no wonder the first names are not the same ones,
For these were their children, or else their grandsons.
'Twas forty long years since the child slaves got free.
We are lacking all proof of the family trees.

What was passed down was an outlook on life.
You fend for yourselves, and look out for your neighbors.
This was the start of the hillbilly culture,
Descendants of those who were forced into labor. [416]

PART FOUR

XLI.

In the colony of Maryland, in regard to slavery,
There was no opposition until seventeen and eighty,
Not in public anyway, or ever written down.
Abolitionists were always underground.

English common law reveals the reason
Why the record shows no public opposition.
Such an act was not exactly treason,
But the judges could construe this as sedition.

To incite the subjects of the king, except by lawful means,
With intent to alter anything the church or state established,
To encourage discontent, or disturbance of the peace,
Or to promote hostility between the social classes,

An Act of sixteen sixty one defined these as sedition.
One was not to criticize the Parliament or King,
Or be heard to utter words not to their liking,
And it became "seditious libel" if in writing.

The king can do no wrong, because he is the king.
Therefore it was wrong to criticize.
It was no defense to prove the words were true,
For truth can be a greater threat than lies.

By the law of Pennsylvania this was not so great a crime.
Sedition there was punished by a fine.
But in the other colonies where common law prevailed,
Offenders could be given life in jail.

And so, in Pennsylvania, the Quakers could speak out.
As to where they stood, they left no room for doubt.
But in Maryland, with nothing on the record for to find,
Historians must read between the lines. [423]

XLII.

In the year of sixteen forty, when Maryland was new,
The Assembly passed a law regarding servants newly freed.
In addition to one axe, two hoes, and freedom corn and clothes,
They would each have fifty acres for their needs.

This could not all be forested, or wetland.
Five acres must be "plantable" for seed.
But Maryland repealed the clause allowing fifty acres,
Retroactively, in sixteen sixty-three.

In Charles County, Maryland, the records are complete.
We have the names of everyone who ever filed a deed.
Of all of the survivors who arrived without indentures,
The free holders numbered only thirty-three.

Twenty-two survivors self-identified as planters.
Eighteen of these were tenants, with no land of their own.
Fifty-eight owned livestock – cattle, hogs, or horses.
Thirty-five of these were tenants, with no land of their own.

One hundred twenty had no land or livestock.
Almost none of these had ever learned a trade.
We only know of their survival to adulthood
Because of court appearances they made.

Six hundred sixty-six who had arrived without indentures
Cannot be accounted for in any public records.
They may have died in servitude, they may have run away,
Or lived quietly unto themselves until their dying day. [429]

XLIII.

What the records reveal is a network.
Survivors looked out for each other,
Bonded by common experience,
As strongly as sisters and brothers.

Fellow survivors protected estates
Of those who died young, in their thirties.
When they "lay very sick" they were "tended and cherished,"
And buried, with tears, when they perished.

They adopted the orphans of former child slaves,
Or anyone's children in need of a home.
Some were abused, and some were abandoned.
Their guardians raised them as ones of their own.

Some of these orphans were bound to survivors
Who now had a skill, and could teach them a trade:
A tanner, a shoemaker, shipwright, or cooper.
A fine set of tools when they went their own way.

We know the survivors engaged in resistance.
To protest in public was never an option.
They did oppose slavery, very directly,
By purchasing children at auction.

No laws were broken, no crime was committed.
They brought them to court to be sentenced.
All this was perfectly workable.
It was never a crime to be merciful.

There only were nine who could ever afford this.
The first, and the youngest, was thirty-nine years.
All had other children, by birth or adoption,
With room for one more, from the auction.

Only one of the nine who were rescued appears
In the records for subsequent years.
His name was John Cole. He became a free man,
Married with children, owner of land.

There are no complaints of abuse or neglect,
Petitions for freedom, or running away.
They all were well treated, or maybe set free
From the prospect of being a slave.

Whatever the case, these nine gallant men
Who survived the ordeal they went through,
Lived by the rule, to do unto them
What you wish had been done unto you. [439]

XLIV.

The "Perpetual Laws of Maryland,"
"Relating to Servants and Slaves,"
Offered two hundred pounds of tobacco
For helping to capture a runaway.

To intimidate open resisters
From harboring runaway servants and slaves,
A fine was provided by law
Of five hundred pounds of tobacco per day.

To put such a fine in perspective,
So that all of us might understand,
Five hundred pounds of tobacco could buy
Twenty-five acres of land.

One who resisted was Edward Darnell.
Baptized in London, sixteen sixty-nine,
At the age of eighteen he was captured and sold
To the worst of all masters, the said Philip Lynes.

Edward Darnell, let the reader remember,
Had come to Court naked one day in November,
Starving from hunger, freezing with cold,
The desperate plea of a tormented soul.

And now, well established, at age thirty-six,
With a wife and four children, and so much to lose,
He sheltered a runaway servant one night,
Knowing what it is like to be badly abused.

So Edward Darnell was indicted,
Entitled to trial by jury,
And the Court, in a highly unusual move,
Appointed for him an attorney.

The Sheriff impaneled a jury
Of men in the court's jurisdiction.
Some were likely to vote for acquittal,
Some were likely to vote for conviction.

One was a Constable. It was his job
To apprehend runaway servants and slaves,
Including his own servant, one year before,
Who was sentenced to five hundred days.

One had embezzled two orphans' estates,
And forced a young cripple three times into court,
Refusing to pay him his corn and his clothes,
One musket, one axe, and two hoes.

One was the son of a man brought to court
For beating and wounding a servant,
And refusing five others their corn and their clothes;
This could not have been inadvertent.

His mother had gifted, as servant for life,
A boy who was from the East Indies.
Soon after this trial the Court set him free,
The son not objecting, for all we can see.

And this is the beauty of trial by jury.
Because a unanimous vote is required,
The hardest of hearts, and the wavering peers,
Can be swayed by the merciful pleas that they hear.

On the jury, as well, were men who adopted
Orphans or fatherless children,
And some who were married, with kids of their own,
And they carried the day when the verdict was known.

So Edward Darnell was a free man again,
And how many other compassionate men
Did shelter, for one night, a runaway slave,
Was a secret they took to their graves. [454]

XLV.

In Charles County, Maryland, in sixty years of records,
There were three hundred runaways recaptured, altogether,
And though they never said where they were going,
We have evidence. We do have ways of knowing.

The inlets of the Chesapeake are in between peninsulas.
The runaways could not have crossed from one onto the next.
Fifteen escaped the province, but were captured in Virginia,
Which is how we know they all were heading west.

They had to get beyond where Harpers Ferry is today,
And crossing the Potomac just above the Shenandoah,
They were now beyond the reach of British law,
In a valley that the white man seldom saw.

There were landmarks as they made their way to freedom.
Above the falls of the Potomac they could walk along the shore
Until, at last, they passed through stupendous water gaps
Where the mountains rise a thousand feet or more.

If they followed the meanders of the Shenandoah River
To the North Fork where Front Royal is today,
On beyond the Cedar Creek, and round the Sandy Hook,
A well established path would guide their way.

The Shenandoah Hunting Path, the Appalachian Warriors' Path,
By both names it was known, and with good reason.
Along the tributary streams that flow to the Potomac,
Tribal warriors dwelt in winter season.

In summer months they hunted in the Shenandoah Valley,
From the banks of the Potomac to the branches of the Holston.
A hunting path developed that was used for trading missions,
And oftentimes for warlike expeditions.

But runaways were safer here, beyond the Blue Ridge Mountains,
Where the British thought no white man ever ventured,
Thinking no one would be brave enough to live among the tribes,
Least of all a child without indentures.

But the Shenandoah Valley is four hundred miles in length,
And the villages of tribes were widely scattered.
By all accounts, the warriors left white settlers undisturbed
In the hollows of the mountains where they gathered. [463]

XLVI.

Of all recaptured runaways at Charles County Court,
There were only thirty-eight without indentures,
Which begs the question: Why not seek more volunteers,
Instead of nabbing children and enslaving them for years?

By the time they ran away, nearly all were in their twenties.
The youngest one was all of seventeen.
He was gone for thirty-seven days, and sentenced to a year,
And nowhere in the records does he ever more appear.

By the time they ran away, they were many years enslaved,
Most of them for four to seven years.
Six had served a longer time, eleven years at best,
Before their masters forced them to confess,

But those cases are not quite as they appear.
They were brought to Court upon the eve of freedom,
And sentenced to as much as three years more,
For absences of many years before.

There were some who could not wait to run away.
Oftentimes the reason why is plain.
One was absent sixty days within his first three months.
He was servant to the mother of John Bayne.

Another ran away in two years' time.
He was servant to the evil Philip Lines.
They sentenced him to nineteen months, and then,
When he had the chance, he ran away again.

Sometimes servants ran away in groups.
The Charles County records furnish proof.
Five who ran away from Philip Lines
Were brought back into Court all at one time.

This happened other times, surely eight or nine.
They were heading toward a wilderness unknown,
And though they did not know what they would find,
They knew they could not make it on their own.

But there were published stories of the Shenandoah Valley.
The geography was vaguely understood.
If they could find the trails the explorers had discovered,
They could safely disappear into the woods. [472]

XLVII.

Abraham Wood, in the year of sixteen fifty,
Crossed the Blue Ridge into the Shenandoah Valley,
And the most important thing to be considered
Is that he discovered westward flowing rivers.

While exploring with a little group of five,
Four white men and an Appomattoc guide,
They had crossed the watershed divide,
The first white men to see the other side.

There were many explorations in the course of twenty years.
The journals that he published brought him fame,
And the river that he found within the Shenandoah Valley
For a hundred years or more did bear his name.

Thomas Batts and Robert Fallam went downriver
To the Narrows at the edge of West Virginia,
Where the mountains rise a thousand feet and more
On either side, above the winding shore.

From there they climbed up high upon the mountain,
Which they explored as far southwestward as it goes.
Some say they found the Tug Fork, the border of Kentucky,
But this is farther than the Fallam journal shows. [477]

XLVIII.

'Twas early in spring, sixteen seventy three,
When James Needham and Gabriel Arthur,
With Indian guides and a team of four horses,
Set out to explore even farther.

Ascending to Yadkin headwaters,
Traversing the source of the New,
Crossing the Blue Ridge in North Carolina,
The Indians knew the way through.

Gazing below from the Blowing Rock,
Retracing the Trail of the Bear,
Bypassing Grandfather Mountain,
The Indians led the way there.

Through Brushy Creek Gap to the North Toe,
To the river they call Nolichucky,
And high on a bluff at a sharp river bend
Stood a Cherokee village at long journey's end.

James Needham left Gabriel Arthur behind.
He was murdered and never returned,
And Gabriel Arthur was tied to a stake,
And as he was about to be burned,

The chief of the Cherokees came to his rescue,
A gun on his shoulder, a knife in his hand.
He shot the assailant, cut Gabriel loose,
And adopted the grateful young man.

He promised to carry him home to Virginia
If he would obey their commands for one year,
And help them to plunder and pillage
A number of enemy villages.

Gabriel Arthur was just twenty-two.
Armed with a hatchet, a knife, and a gun,
He joined in the raids of both Spanish and English,
With greater adventure to come.

A party of sixty would raid the Shawnee
On the banks of the river they call the Ohio,
A distance of three hundred miles, maybe more,
Where never a white man had journeyed before.

They followed the forks of the Holston,
And the valley that leads to Wood River.
It is now called New River, but I disagree,
For the river itself is as old as can be.

The river meanders are deeply incised,
Older than all of the plateaus and ridges.
As mountains were ever so slowly uplifted,
The New River valley was deepened, not shifted.

Leaving the valley they call Shenandoah,
The river cuts right through two parallel mountains,
And there, near the mouth of Spruce Run,
Caves in the limestone could shelter someone.

Through the Valleys and Ridges the river meanders,
With banks never less than one hundred feet high,
Until, at the Narrows, the slopes are so steep,
And the gap is quite nearly two thousand feet deep.

This is the last of the parallel ridges.
Beyond is the vast Allegheny Plateau,
Deeply dissected by countless ravines,
Where the mountains are remnants, left in between.

This is the start of the New River Gorge,
Which never is less than five hundred feet deep.
When joined by the Bluestone, and then the Greenbrier,
The sides of the gorge are much higher.

After passing the Kanawha Falls,
The gorge is still deep, but the flood plain is wide.
Buffalo traces were easily followed
Downriver, along either side.

The Cherokee stayed with the Moneton tribe
A day's journey from the Ohio.
They crossed the Big Sandy to raid the Shawnee
At the mouth of the river Scioto.

And Gabriel Arthur, a white man, had traveled
This far from the river they call Nolichucky,
The first to traverse what is now West Virginia,
The first to set foot in Kentucky. [495]

XLIX.

On the mouth of the river Scioto,
Where it empties into the Ohio,
The Cherokee raiders upon the Shawnee
Were bravely repulsed by their enemy.

Gabriel Arthur could make no escape.
Shot in his thigh with an arrow,
He was taken a prisoner there,
And they noticed the length of his hair.

Cherokee warriors cut their hair short
So their enemies could not take hold.
They scrubbed off his war paint, and to their delight,
They saw that the young man was white.

They admired his knife and his hatchet,
And had never before seen a gun.
They showed him a beaver they lately had killed,
And Gabriel Arthur, so clever and skilled,

Offered to bring them more weapons,
Which he would exchange for their furs.
They gave him some corn, and they left him his gun,
And they let him go back to from where he had come.

But not by the route he had taken,
For this was unknown to Shawnee.
Where Cabin Creek meets the Ohio,
The young man was likely set free.

This was the well defined "Warrior's Path."
On the map of John Filson a century later,
With numerous stream crossings showing,
We can see where the young man was going.

Venturing southward up Indian Run,
Crossing the Sap Branch at Battle Run,
Crossing the Licking at Upper Blue Licks,
The trail of the buffalo led him to this.

Down Lulbegrud Creek to Red River,
Across the Kentucky at Station Camp Creek,
Up the War Fork, and across Sturgeon Creek,
Across Sexton Creek, and up the Goose Creek,

Up Otter Creek, and down the Trace Fork
To Flat Lick and Cumberland River,
Fording the river at Pine Mountain Gap,
Up Big Yellow Creek to the Cumberland Gap.

This is the singular pass through a mountain
One hundred miles long with a thousand foot rise.
The southeastern slopes are relentlessly steep,
But the Cumberland Gap is alluring and deep.

The Warriors Path followed eastward from here
Across the Clinch River, through Moccasin Gap,
Across the North Fork of the Holston,
To the valley they call Shenandoah.

Gabriel Arthur had been here before.
He turned south at the Holston and found Nolichucky,
The very first white man who ever had crossed
What we now call the State of Kentucky.

He did this alone, then he found his way home,
Escorted by Cherokee, true to their word.
He related the story to Abraham Wood,
Who put it in writing as well as he could.

Received by John Locke, and endorsed in his hand,
The story soon spread of these wondrous new lands,
Where buffalo trails could be followed with ease,
Where pioneer settlers could live as they please. [510]

L.

Among the first settlers beyond the Blue Ridge
Were runaway servants from Maryland.
Some of their names were uncommon enough
To be tracked by a careful comparison.

Runaways rarely were brought before Court
Till the year of sixteen eighty one,
Till the government offered a handsome reward
For capturing those who had run.

If they ran away once, they might run away twice,
From the years added on to their sentence.
No records survive of these runaways' lives,
But we sometimes can find their descendants.

The very same surnames can often be found
Where one would expect for to find them
Near the Potomac, beyond the Blue Ridge,
With the coastal plantations behind them.

Not all of the runaways crossed the Potomac.
Some stayed in Maryland, on the north side,
Past all the water gaps, past the Blue Ridge,
Where they knew they could easily hide.

The last water gap is one thousand feet deep,
And eight miles beyond it is Antietam Creek,
Which flows through the valley behind the South Mountain,
Where no one could ever have found them.

Some of the runaways settled right here.
Gabby and Moats are two names that appear
On the earliest tax list for Antietam Creek.
These are two names that were almost unique.

These were descendants of runaway servants.
And the names of another eleven are found
On the very same tax list, the very first census,
Or records of marriage, on Maryland ground.

Bacon and Burditt, Line and Munroe,
Appear on the tax list as well,
But the names of their fathers and mothers,
None of the records can tell.

Bayhan and Cheston, Collum and Bunn,
Lackey and Gauff and Magraw,
Their ancestors likely were runaway servants,
Beyond the long arm of the law.

Six of these names were on Lower Antietam,
Where runaways first found their freedom.
When the century turned, all the others were gone.
They got married, or died, or moved on. [521]

LI.

Beyond the Blue Ridge Mountains, where now is Harpers Ferry,
Where the Shenandoah enters the Potomac,
The river it is shallow, with rocky, sandy shoals.
Runaways could cross on rafts, pushing them with poles.

They could settle on the flood plain of the Shenandoah River,
With the nearest Shawnee village safely sixteen miles away,
Or follow either fork from where Front Royal is today,
To the Shenandoah Valley or the limestones of Luray.

When all these servants ran away there was no county here.
They lived without a government as long as fifty years.
By seventeen and forty three it all was Frederick County,
But the runaways had long since disappeared.

When the tax men made the rounds in seventeen and forty four,
Taking names of settlers, knocking on the cabin doors,
There were sons of runaways who still were hunkered down.
John Crowson and John Harrold were the only ones they found.

Near to the Potomac, in what now is West Virginia,
Many of the surnames of the runaways are listed,
In the early marriage records, or in the census records,
And their families have forgotten they existed.

Butterfield and Bacon, Maddock and McKenny,
Cusick and Crowson, Varley, Todd and Ware,
Lackey, Goel and Jeffries, Goddard and Rigby,
The surnames of these runaways were there.

Most of them were married in what then was Berkeley County,
And their movements can be tracked across the land.
A few were never more than twenty miles from Harpers Ferry.
The rest found greener pastures at command.

Some passed by Fort Cumberland and crossed the Alleghanies,
Traveling by pack horse or by Conestoga wagon,
Emerging on the farmland of Monongahela Valley,
Looking for a place to build a cabin.

Some continued all the way to Wheeling, West Virginia,
Where the turnpike reached the banks of the Ohio.
In the valley of Muskingum they could settle down at last,
Or they could float downriver on a raft. [530]

LII.

In days long ago when our nation was young,
When the long revolution was over and done,
We set our sights westward and followed the sun,
Exploring the lands we had recently won.

The roads through the mountains were crude and remote.
It was simpler and safer to buy a flat boat
Or a raft made of logs so the family could float
Down the river they call the Ohio.

On the upper Ohio the sand bars kept shifting,
Stopping the rafts and the flat boats from drifting,
So migrating families trekked onward to Wheeling
And hazards the deep waters there were concealing.

The upper Ohio was forest primeval,
With branches extending out over the waters,
With glistening rapids and sweeping meanders.
No one had ever seen anything grander.

The cut banks on one side reached up to the sky,
Sometimes as much as four hundred feet high.
On the opposite shores, where the slopes were not steep,
Alluvial soils were both fertile and deep.

Migrating families venturing there
With their wood stoves and beds, and their tables and chairs,
And their animals crammed on a flat boat or raft,
Would float down the river and never come back.

With a pull at the oars they might stay in the current,
But sometimes at flood stage the river was swift,
With treacherous whirlpools to draw the boat in,
And water too high to pass underneath limbs.

Whenever the banks of the river caved in,
Tree roots would sink and be captured within,
With the broken tops oftentimes hidden from view,
To puncture a boat as it tried to pass through.

But most of the voyaging families were lucky,
And entered a paradise known as Kentucky,
With bountiful orchards of wild nuts and berries,
Crab apples, plums, and wild grapes, and wild cherries,

Flowers so beautiful, meadows so green,
Trees as gigantic as ever were seen,
Plentiful fish in the clear mountain streams,
And deer in the forest, it felt like a dream. [540]

LIII.

In colonial Virginia, when first the white man came,
All the early settlements were on the coastal plain.
Nearly all were Englishmen, by birth and pedigree,
Their destinies decided by the lords across the sea.

Behind them was the Blue Ridge, as far as could be seen.
The passes through the mountain range were few and far between.
Beyond was the "Back Country," which the white men seldom saw,
Where settlement had always been prohibited by law.

Beyond the Blue Ridge Mountains was the Shenandoah Valley,
One hundred sixty miles from the Potomac to the James,
Burned over by the Indians, as meadow for wild game.
Many tribes would visit there to hunt, but not remain.

The hunting path extended to the waters of the Holston,
With branches to what now are West Virginia and Kentucky.
By the time Virginia issued grants to settle on these lands,
Squatters staked their claims and built log cabins with their hands.

Scattered far and wide throughout the Shenandoah Valley,
And clustered where New River enters into West Virginia,
And at the Holston River where a trail led to Kentucky,
Are found in early records if one takes the time to study,

More than thirty surnames of the runaways from Maryland,
Migrating further westward as new counties formed around them,
Passing through the Gap into the Cumberland Plateau,
On the Warrior's Path, or the Wilderness Road,

To the Cumberland River, across from Cherokee,
Or on the Warrior's Path, at the ford of the Kentucky,
Or along the Stoner Creek, or on the Buffalo Trace,
Or on the road to Lexington, or on the Logan Trace.

In a missionary's journal is a telling episode.
When he emerged onto the bluegrass from the Wilderness Road,
He rode down to Crab Orchard, and found company enough.
Some of them were wild, and some of them were rough.

Some of them were drunkards, and some of them were liars.
They used abusive language, and they cursed him to his face.
Before he made it safely through he heard a pistol fired
From the hills above Dick's River, overlooking Logan Trace.

Some of the descendants of the runaways were here,
At Crab Orchard, in Kentucky, where they settled the frontier.
There were many other settlers where the rivers all flow west.
On the shoulders of them all our nation's western claims would rest.

In the bluegrass there were barons who had papers granting title.
They could not defeat the claims made good by axe and plough and rifle,
Of families who had lived in western hills for generations,
Who knew how to survive within the woods, in isolation.

The Spanish, French, and English had designs upon this land,
But they had no one to claim it, build a house, and make their stand.
These were true Americans, who made Kentucky home,
Not to be moved by any government, least of all their own. [552]

LIV.

It was just a hundred years ago,
It has not been so very long,
When scholars roamed the Kentucky hills,
Searching for the old folk songs.

They rode the train to the Cumberland Gap,
And onward to the Pineville Station,
At the water gap of the Warriors' Path,
On the edge of civilization.

The pioneers had been living here
Since the early days of our nation,
And they passed on the old folk songs
To the younger generations.

But for the hymns they sung at church,
These were the only songs they heard.
And every song would tell a story.
They learned them word for word.

Deep within the mountain valleys,
Apart from all the modern world,
Their spoken words distinctly ancient,
Even those of boys and girls.

When song collectors came a-knocking,
The singers all would share their songs,
And children sometimes sang it for them
If the grownups got it wrong.

The songs were from the north of England,
And from the lowlands of Scotland.
The family trees are rooted there,
Though the lines are long forgotten.

Their ancestors who sailed the seas,
Some of them were refugees,
Some were servants with indentures,
Some were looking for adventure.

On the Poor Fork below Pine Mountain
Lived a boy named Tilford Creech.
Somehow the song collectors found him,
Fourteen miles up the creek.

He sang a song from ancient Scotland
From the seventeenth century,
To the haunting tune that you're hearing now,
And he sang it from memory.

His father's father, and his mother's mother,
Were first cousins to each other.
Both were grandchildren of Enoch Creech,
And that was the family tree.

No one knows from whence they came.
But the first time we find the name
Is in the year of sixteen sixty one,
A kidnapped child from London.

Some of those who took to the hills
Were brought here quite against their will,
Sold as slaves, and they ran away
To a mountain hideaway.

For if they spoke with a Scottish brogue,
They might be heard on the open road.
But the Appalachian Mountains hid them,
And they brought their folk songs with them. [566]

LV.

There was another way for runaways to find their way to freedom.
They could navigate their way to Pennsylvania.
All they needed was a raft, or any vessel that would float,
But what they really wanted was a boat.

Once they were out upon the bay, they could surely find their way,
Northward to the Susquehanna River,
With Mennonites on one side, Scots-Irish on the other,
From their bondage they would surely be delivered.

The reader will remember that the Mennonites and Quakers,
In Germantown, in sixteen eighty eight,
Were the first to protest slavery in written words on paper,
Though only four men signed it on that date.

It was only five years later when George Keith, another Quaker,
Was quoting Deuteronomy, twenty-three fifteen:
Thou shalt not deliver to his master any servant
Escaping from his master unto thee.

He said that Christ had died not only to save souls,
But also to deliver the oppressed,
To bring "liberty both inward and outward."
He was putting their religion to the test.

This was in the very year, in sixteen ninety three,
When the Quakers started buying kids from Scotland.
Not till seventeen and ten did the last of these get free,
But the words the Quakers heard were not forgotten.

Pennsylvania passed a tariff, in seventeen and twelve,
Twenty pounds for every Negro slave imported.
This interference with the slave trade was rescinded by the Queen.
Nonetheless, the opposition was recorded.

It started with the Mennonites of Germantown,
Who were disturbed that Quaker friends had Negro slaves,
The Mennonites preferred to do their labor on their own,
And they raised their many children the same way.

This brings us back to Maryland, to Charles County Court,
Where three hundred captured runaways were sentenced.
All but four of them were white, and we may not know their plight,
But we know that most of them were unrepentant.

If they ran away again, we do not know where or when,
Except for one occasion, when we do.
They might have sung this shanty as they rowed their way to freedom,
In August, seventeen and thirty two. [576]

LVI.

Row, boys, row! To the north we go!
Traveling by night, and in the day laying low!
Row, boys, row! To the north we go!
Off to Pennsylvania and the Quakers!

Four slave boys are we, or so we used to be,
But we are never going back-O!
We've got a boat, and a promissory note
To fetch a big load of tobacco!

And it's row, boys, row! To the north we go!
Traveling by night, and in the day laying low!
Row, boys, row! To the north we go!
Off to Pennsylvania and the Quakers!

We've got a boat, and such a big boat
It takes four lads for to row it!
We'll be away, out upon the bay,
Before the master ever knows it!

And it's row, boys, row! To the north we go!
Traveling by night, and in the day laying low!
Row, boys, row! To the north we go!
Off to Pennsylvania and the Quakers!

He'll lose his nerve, and he'll get what he deserves
When he finally figures out he'll never catch us!
He'll be down on his knees, begging if you please,
Have mercy, I can't pay my taxes!

And it's row, boys, row! To the north we go!
Traveling by night, and in the day laying low!
Row, boys, row! To the north we go!
Off to Pennsylvania and the Quakers!

O, they'll take is in, for they know it's not a sin,
And we'll be free forever after!
And we'll settle down, on our own plots of ground,
And we will call no man master!

And it's row, boys, row! To the north we go!
Traveling by night, and in the day laying low!
Row, boys, row! To the north we go!
Off to Pennsylvania and the Quakers! [585]

PART FIVE

LVII.

Kids who were captured in Ireland, England, or Scotland,
Transported across the Atlantic and sold into slavery,
Could never go home, they had no way to pay for the passage,
If they ever got free from their treatment so brutal and savage.

But those who were taken from out on the coast of New England
Were on the same side of the ocean as when they were kids,
And if they completed their sentence were free to go home.
They could walk all the way if they had to, and some of them did.

For there was a pathway connecting the towns on the Fall Line,
And it followed the New England coast the full distance to Boston,
A crude riding trail meant for carrying mail on a horse.
Though a long way to walk, it was easy to follow the course.

In colonial days it was called **the Queen's Road or King's Highway**,
With bridges and ferries where passage might not have been free,
And forts on the rivers protecting the British frontier,
It was not a safe place for a runaway servant to be.

For instance, James Hambleton, nine generations before me,
Kidnapped at seventeen years from the province of Maine,
Sold as a "servant" in Westmoreland County, Virginia,
Adjudged to be twelve, he was punished because of his name.

The son of a rebel, a prisoner taken by Cromwell,
He was sentenced to twelve years of slavery, rather than five.
He tried to go home and was captured out on the King's Highway,
And more than a year and a half was tacked onto his time.

He ended up married with children in northern Virginia.
He had family in Maine, and he never did see them again.
But there were homecomings of servants who had no indentures,
And the long journey back to their homes was a major adventure. [592]

LVIII.

Of all of the kids from the coast of New England,
Sold off as slaves at the Chesapeake Bay,
Who found their way home when their nightmare was over,
No one had farther to walk than John Bray.

He grew up in Gloucester, northeast Massachusetts,
Was kidnapped from there at thirteen years of age,
Brought before Court in York County, Virginia,
And these are the words written down on the page.

He was "imported," that is the word,
In a ship called the "Phillipp" by one Henry Creeke,
Sold as a slave to a man named John Huberd,
Nine years to serve him, and then to be free.

Further research tells us who these men were.
There were other white slave ships in Henry's career.
He commanded the "Hercules," also the "Hannah,"
Over the space of ten barbarous years.

John Huberd died soon, and the record does show
Who got the cattle, but not the child slave.
We do know the dead man's estate was appraised
By one Otto Thorpe and his partner John Page.

These men were major child traffickers,
Who owned the white slave ship called "Planters Adventure."
Between them, they owned, in York County, Virginia,
Twenty white children who had no indentures.

John Huberd's brother, the records report,
Had once been a Justice at York County Court.
As were Otto Thorpe, and his partner John Page
During some of the years that John Bray was a slave.

When John Bray got free, all a servant was owed,
By custom, not law, was a new suit of clothes,
And some bushels of corn which he probably sold
To have coins in his pocket while out on the road.

He would not have had anything else to his name,
Not even a rifle to shoot at wild game,
But if questioned, wherever he happened to be,
He had a court record to prove he was free.

He had seven hundred long miles for to walk,
And more than a dozen wide rivers to cross,
Before his own family would burst into tears,
To lay eyes on their boy who'd been gone for nine years.

Maybe he stopped at some farms on the way,
And offered to labor for one or two days,
In exchange for a meal, or to sleep in the hay.
Guardian angels protected John Bray.

He made it to Gloucester, with no earthly guide.
His mother and father were both still alive.
His siblings were living there, four of the five.
In another two years he would marry his bride.

His parents were married sixteen forty six.
Written right into the record is this:
His father, of Gloucester, by name Thomas Bray,
Was a "ship carpenter," that was his trade.

This explains why his boy had been down at the docks.
While watching the ships he was easily caught,
Or lured upon board, and they sailed away with him,
And made him a kidnapping victim. [606]

LIX.

In the town of Scituate, the Massachusetts shore,
Thirty Pilgrims landed there in sixteen thirty four,
And they rejoiced to find there, after jail time in "The Clink,"
A church without a bishop and a state without a king.

One of them was Samuel House, an in-law of the minister.
He had a son named Samuel, and a daughter named Elizabeth,
Who both had many children in the space of twenty years,
And both of them had sons who disappeared.

The elder Samuel House was a ship carpenter by trade,
And the skill was handed down within the family.
John Sutton Junior, who was married to Elizabeth,
Was likewise a ship carpenter at Scituate.

John the Third, their eldest son, born sixteen sixty four,
Disappeared one fateful day from down upon the shore.
In Talbot County, Maryland, John Sutton's name appears,
Ordered by the Court to be a slave for seven years.

No one knew what happened until sixteen eighty six,
When he returned a free man and could tell them all of this.
His parents, his four sisters, and three brothers all were living,
But John House, his younger cousin, had gone missing.

If only he had made it home a few short months before,
He might have warned his cousin of the danger on the shore,
But John House was on the Rappahannock River in Virginia,
Ordered into servitude for twelve years by the Court.

While John was in captivity, his uncle Samuel died.
His son and then his nephew had been taken on his watch.
The fault lay with the pirates, but he may have blamed himself,
For having looked away while either boy was at the docks. [613]

LX.

John Pearson lived in Rowley, in northeastern Massachusetts.
The son of Jeremiah, and the grandson of the Deacon,
Near the port of Ipswich on the Plum Island Sound,
And the sailing ships, the captains, and the seamen.

Family legend has it that when John was only twelve
To the Caribbean Sea he bravely sailed,
Where he narrowly escaped being captured by the pirates,
And he somehow made it home to tell the tale.

The family has no record to substantiate the story,
But legends often have a grain of truth.
There is a record in Virginia that is not so full of glory,
Of what happened to John Pearson as a youth.

At just about this time, in sixteen ninety-nine,
At Henrico County Court his name appears.
He was only nine years old, but they thought he was eleven,
And they ordered him to serve for thirteen years.

His expected date of freedom was in seventeen and twelve,
And by this time, Virginia law had changed.
Besides his "freedom corn," he was entitled to a rifle,
And also thirty shillings pocket change.

He was somewhere near to Richmond, in Virginia,
At least six hundred miles away from home,
So he set out on the highway, and he headed for New England,
And he had to make the journey all alone.

He would cross the Rappahannock and Potomac,
The Susquehanna, Delaware and Hudson,
And walk the Boston Post Road into Stonington, Connecticut,
And there he found a woman who would love him.

Her name it was Elizabeth, and she was twenty-two.
Less than two years later they would marry.
At first they lived in Stonington, five miles from Rhode Island,
And then moved near to Rowley, at Newbury.

Elizabeth was only thirty-seven when she died,
The mother of eight children, only six of whom survived.
But John lived to be ninety, and with rebel flag unfurled,
He lived to hear the "shot heard round the world."

John Pearson had four grandsons who were soldiers
When they were not running grist and lumber mills.
Amos Pearson, son of Silas, was a minuteman.
He was wounded, early on, at Bunker Hill.

Among the stolen children who returned to Massachusetts,
Twenty had descendants who were in the Revolution.
As history records, there was "a long train of abuses,"
But they may have fought, in part, for retribution,

Especially the grandsons of John Pearson,
Who heard him tell his tale when they were children,
Before it got passed down through generations,
With embellishment and much exaggeration.

He did not escape the pirates on the sailing ships.
It is well that we should call them what they were.
They were selling stolen children into slavery.
This is piracy, there is no better word. [626]

LXI.

Thomas Hewett was an orphan boy from Hingham, Massachusetts.
His father died when he was ten, his mother five years after.
The oldest of five children, and they did have next of kin.
There were many aunts and uncles, we don't know who took them in.

Perhaps he was a vagrant child, an orphan on his own.
Thomas Hewett ended up five hundred miles from home,
At County Court in Rappahannock County in Virginia,
At the tender age of sixteen years, and not yet fully grown.

His master, Thomas Taylor, had no children of his own.
He displayed unto the orphan boy a mercy seldom shown.
He agreed in open Court to teach the boy to read and write.
But things did not work out as Thomas Hewett hoped they might.

It was only three years afterward that Thomas Taylor died.
All we know about him is his will, which has survived.
These are his very words, if one reads through it:
"I clearly discharge and set free my boy, Thomas Huitt."

And he gave to him his wool and linen clothes
To protect him from the sun and from the snows.
He left his coins and his tobacco all to others.
Thomas now was free, but he never did recover.

His body made it home, the record shows,
But his suffering was more than we can know.
History describes the boy as nothing other than
"An unfortunate insane young man." [632]

LXII.

Benjamin Smith was a fatherless child.
His father was drowned in a shipwreck,
Retreating to Boston with New England troops
After failing to capture Quebec.

As they entered the Gulf of Saint Lawrence,
The fleet sailed right into a storm,
And sank off the coast of Cape Breton,
Leaving none but the sea gulls to mourn.

Lieutenant James Smith was the father,
With a wife and six children behind.
This was in sixteen and ninety,
When Benjamin Smith was just nine.

At Newbury port on the New England shore
His father was there to protect him no more
In sixteen ninety nine he was carried away
To Charles County Court on the Chesapeake Bay.

Adjudged as nineteen, he had six years to serve.
He was younger than that, so it could have been worse.
His master, who owned him, was one William Dent,
A Major, by then, and a very rich gent.

He had six thousand acres of land,
He served as Provincial Attorney,
Was an Officer in the king's Navy,
While Benjamin Smith was in slavery.

One of his "servants" was Turlough O'Bryan,
Kidnapped from somewhere in Ireland,
Who came into Court to complain
That he had been treated with violence.

William Willson was his overseer
Whom the "servants" had reason to fear.
Turlough O'Bryan accused him
Of abusing and beating and wounding him.

The man who did prosecute every defendant
Was Willson's employer, the said William Dent,
Who was also the master of Turlough O'Bryan.
The case went to trial, and here's how it went.

There were witnesses sworn and examined and heard,
Who told what they saw in their very own words.
William Wilson was thereby found guilty and fined
For what he had done to young Turlough O'Bryan.

Frances Hogg was a young girl from Stepney, in London.
Kidnappers caught her, and William Dent bought her.
Over the course of her first three years' time,
She fell in love with young Turlough O'Bryan.

William Dent gave them permission to wed,
Split the difference in time still remaining to serve,
So they both would be free on the very same day,
With clothing and shillings, to go their own way.

Not all the masters were monsters.
They could, on occasion, be kind.
Servants were property, purchased and sold,
But abuse, if severe, was a crime.

Benjamin Smith never did run away,
Or complain of abuse or neglect,
Or have need to petition for freedom,
But he was, as are all slaves, oppressed.

He made it back home, and he married a wife,
Had four sons and three daughters, and lived a short life,
Only forty-one years, and his stone can be found
At Newbury port, in the burying ground.

He had ten descendants who served in the war.
Seven were minutemen, risking their lives
At Lexington, Concord or Cambridge
On the nineteenth of April, in seventeen seventy five. [648]

LXIII.

Isabel Hay was a Scottish girl.
Her father was from Scotland.
And she was born in Charlestown,
A few short miles from Boston.

Her mother died when she was two.
Her father did remarry.
She had two older siblings.
Their names were James and Mary.

Two half-brothers, two half-sisters
Whom she did love so dear,
And then, in seventeen o eight,
Isabel disappeared.

She was not yet seventeen,
And still a fair young maid.
They shipped her off to Maryland,
And sold her as a slave.

Not till six years afterward,
When nearly twenty-three,
And she had served her sentence,
Was Isabel finally free.

She had next to nothing,
And would walk the roads alone,
From the banks of the Wicomico,
Five hundred miles from home.

Unless she sold her freedom corn,
Likewise her axe and hoes,
She had not a shilling
In the pockets of her clothes.

One suit of woven wool,
One shift of new white linen,
One pair of shoes and stockings,
Were all that she was given.

Staying west of the Patuxent,
She had forty miles to go
Before she reached the highway
At Upper Marlborough.

She made it home to Charlestown.
The next year was her wedding
To one Nathaniel Nichols,
Born and raised at Reading.

They had children born in Reading,
And some in Framingham,
And more than one descendant
Would become a minuteman.

Six grandsons all were soldiers,
And one granddaughter's husband.
Two of them were minutemen,
Who marched whenever summoned.

One was Jonathan Nichols,
Who marched with Thomas Eaton
From Reading unto Concord,
Where the British troops were beaten.

One was Thomas Damon
Who likewise marched from Reading,
Where the house built by his father
Is still, to this day, standing.

They all converged at Concord,
Some sixteen miles away.
They changed the course of history
Upon that fateful day.

Isabel Hay had long since passed,
But she instilled within them,
Resentment of the British rule,
And a burning love of freedom. [664]

LXIV.

Thomas Walkup was a Scottish boy.
His father was from Scotland.
And he was born in Framingham,
Twenty miles from Boston.

One day when he was nine years old,
Naïve as he could be,
Pirates lured him on their ship
And swept him out to sea.

They shipped him to Virginia,
And sold him as a slave,
With fifteen years the sentence
That the County judges gave.

They called these judges "gentlemen"
In sixteen ninety eight,
Condemning helpless children
To a cruel and heartless fate.

Pulling stumps and plowing fields
In hot Virginia sun,
Harvesting tobacco
From dawn till day was done.

Such was life on the plantation
For a Scot in slavery.
Not till he was twenty-four
Was Thomas Walkup free.

His family passed the legend on
A full three hundred years,
A boy who loved the sailing ships,
And one day disappeared.

They neither witnessed the abduction
Nor saw the ship set sail,
But Thomas Walkup made it home,
Alive, to tell the tale.

He had a wife named Hannah,
And five children who were older
Than the youngest, Thomas Junior,
Who was born to be a soldier.

He was at Fort Massachusetts
And the Fort at Number Four,
Protecting the frontier
In what they call King George's War.

He was home for six or seven years,
And watched his father die,
At the age of sixty-six,
In seventeen and fifty five.

The elder Thomas lived to see
The birth of grandson Francis.
Thomas Junior then enlisted
Once again, and took his chances

In the Crown Point Expedition,
And the Battle of Lake George,
Where he survived an ambush
In a narrow mountain gorge.

He had fought the French and Indians,
And almost lost his life.
He went home to Massachusetts,
To his children and his wife.

It was in the Town of Marlborough
Where Francis came of age.
He heard the Lexington Alarm
Of the advance of General Gage.

Francis was a minuteman
Of firm resolve and will.
He marched to Concord and to Lexington,
And then to Bunker Hill.

These were men who knew their rights,
And knowing, dared defend them,
Whoever the invader
Or aggressor who would end them.

For the Walkups, it was personal.
The family all resisted.
Before the war was over,
Eight more of them had enlisted.

What the British did to Thomas
Was enough to join the fray.
They knew all about it.
They still speak of it today. [683]

LXV.

Thomas Wheeler was a boy of seventeen,
Born and raised in Concord, Massachusetts.
His father was a writer and a soldier,
But the boy was to be put to other uses.

Transported to the seacoast of Virginia,
To be six years a slave on Wallop's Island,
Cut off from the mainland by a mile or more of wetlands,
There was no escape, or any use in trying.

Captain John Wallop was the owner of the island.
He had seven thousand acres altogether,
Was a Justice on the Court, and he owned five children,
And one of them he sentenced at his pleasure.

Timothy Weyley was a motherless child.
His mother died when he was only nine.
Born in Massachusetts, in the little town of Reading,
And he had no idea where he was heading.

To Talbot County, Maryland at Reeds Creek,
Where the Choptank opens to the Chesapeake,
Six years a servant to Nicholas Holmes,
The only child slave he ever owned.

William Hagar was twice enslaved.
Born in Watertown, seven miles from Boston,
Thought to be fourteen, he was sold as a slave
In Charles County, Maryland, at auction.

Seven years later, when the boy got free,
He was nearly eighteen, and no older.
Impressed into service in King Philip's War,
He was forced against his will to be a soldier.

Thomas and Timothy and William
Made it back to Massachusetts and their homes.
It took a little while, but they all got married,
And they lived to see their children fully grown.

Watertown is twelve miles from Concord,
And Reading only sixteen miles away.
Twenty-five of their descendants would turn up there
When it mattered, on a most historic day. [692]

LXVI.

Under cover of darkness on April eighteen,
Crossing in boats, hoping not to be seen,
Eight hundred soldiers with red coats convened,
Preparing to march on to Lexington Green.

We all know the story, recited with pride,
Two lights in the tower, and Paul Revere's ride,
Arriving at midnight, or right about then,
To rouse the militia and all minutemen.

Other riders on horseback were making the rounds
To all of the nearby and outlying towns,
Calling to arms both the old and the young.
Rifles were fired, and alarm bells were rung.

Most of the soldiers lived too far away
To get to the Common before it was day.
A few more than sixty were all that arrived,
Expecting to watch as the British passed by.

Four hundred red coats arrived on the scene,
Grandly parading on Lexington Green.
The rebels were ordered to lay down their arms
And retreat, one and all, to their houses and farms.

But they bravely held on to their rifles instead.
The first British volley went over their heads.
Before they found refuge in forested hills,
Came the next British volley, intended to kill.

As the sun was just rising on April nineteen,
There were eight persons dead upon Lexington Green.
The British troops cheered about what they had done
To a force they outnumbered by seven to one. [699]

LXVII.

Many British officers were seen the night before,
Suspiciously in Lexington, and heading for Concord.
Along the road through Lincoln they arrested Paul Revere,
But other men on horseback were to carry on from here.

To Bedford, and to Concord, and to Acton they did ride,
Alerting all the minutemen throughout the countryside,
And they were all assembled, way up high upon the ridge
Of Punkatasset Hill, and looking down on Concord Bridge.

Advancing to a closer hill, they saw before their eyes
The fires burning down below, the smoke as it did rise.
"To march into the middle of the town for its defense,"
They all resolved to do, or else to "die in the attempt."

As the soldiers turned the corner toward the North Bridge,
Luther Blanchard, playing sweetly on his fife,
Was the first one to be wounded by the British,
His commander, to his rescue, lost his life.

You were not supposed to shoot the musicians,
The only soldiers who were known to be unarmed.
If the minutemen had uniforms, musicians their own color,
Luther Blanchard would have likely been unharmed.

Rifles now were fired in both directions,
And there were dead and wounded on both sides.
The British then retreated to the village,
To wait for reinforcements to arrive.

The British now were eighteen miles from Boston,
And danger would be lurking on the way.
They were granted time to sleep, and this would cost them.
Americans would gather while the British troops delayed.

For more than one mile easterly from Concord,
All along the north side of the road,
The hills rise sixty feet above the valley,
With a commanding view of soldiers down below.

The British troops were ever in the highway,
Marching in formation, wearing uniforms of red.
The Americans were hiding behind walls, or in the houses,
Or among the trees, or high upon a ledge.

Out to Meriam's Corner, where the highway takes a bend,
The Americans had stationed more than fifteen hundred men.
And all the way to Charlestown, until the day was over,
They followed right along and hunted down the British soldiers.

Governments are not replaced for light and transient reasons,
And those who try and fail are charged with treason.
'Twas a long train of abuses caused the British rule to fall,
And the Declaration could not list them all.

Among the soldiers at the North Bridge of Concord,
Caught up in a fight they did not ask for,
And at Meriam's Corner on the Lexington Road,
High upon the ledges, and aiming down below,

Were thirty male descendants of the white child slaves,
Honoring their elders by the choice they made.
Some of them by marriage, and some of them by birth,
And they took a stand for freedom here on earth.

Benjamin Smith and Thomas Wheeler,
Timothy Weyley, William Hagar,
Thomas Walkup and Isabel Hay,
Their spirits all were present on that day.

From Concord, and Acton, and Waltham.
From Chelmsford, and Westford, and Woburn,
From Framingham and Reading, sixteen miles away,
Their descendants fought for liberty that day.

The oldest one was fifty-six, the youngest was sixteen.
The likes of this the world had never seen.
All of them were resolute, upon the battlefield,
To strive, to seek, to find, and not to yield. [715]

LXVIII.

Pay attention now, and gather round,
And hear what is so seldom written down.
History as seen through eyes of children,
One of them from Concord, one from Milton.

There lived a boy of seven, Amos Heald,
Who saw what happened on the battlefield.
He could see the North Bridge on that day,
From his farm house just three hundred yards away.

His father, Daniel Heald, was thirty-five,
And though the muster roll has not survived,
We know he truly was a Concord soldier,
For Amos told the tale when he was older.

He was with his mother on the hill,
Not knowing any soldier would be killed,
Watching the whole battle as it happened.
And at least four of the minutemen from Acton

Also were related to his mother,
And so the family had a lot at stake,
But the world that we shall leave to one another
Depends upon the choices that we make.

There lived a boy named Ebenezer Tucker,
Born in Milton, eight miles south of Boston.
Ebenezer was the oldest of three brothers,
Adventurous, and never known for caution.

His father was a soldier, bearing arms,
The captain of a company of militia,
And when they rang the Lexington Alarm,
Ebenezer wanted to go with them.

"But you're only nine years old," his father said,
"Too young to march with military men."
"I can shoot a British soldier dead."
"I'm old enough," he said, "I'm almost ten."

So Ebenezer Junior marched to Boston,
Joined the siege, and trapped the British there.
He served for seven days, his name is on the page,
No one can deny he did his share.

Perhaps he was a drummer, not a gunner.
The muster roll survives, but does not say.
Children could enlist if with their fathers,
As Ebenezer Junior did that day.

'Tis carved in stone that Ebenezer died
Four months later, almost to the day.
And though the tears have long ago been cried,
He deserves a bronze star on his grave. [726]

EPILOGUE

LXIX.

Let me say it once again, for this is not what we were told.
The British captured little children, many thousand fold,
Forced them onto sailing ships, bound for the plantations,
And sold them into slavery for many years' duration.

They came from Massachusetts, England, Ireland, and Scotland,
Robbed of all their innocence, their liberty, their youth,
And though three hundred years have passed, the story long forgotten,
Let there be no more denial of the documented truth.

And how could such a story go untold?
The children's names are written in the Order Books of old.
And most of them have been transcribed, verbatim, word for word.
Did the scholars never wonder what occurred?

If these were voluntary servants, then why were they in Court?
Why guess their ages, hand down sentences, and write all those reports?
Why will we not acknowledge they were brought against their will?
Does it contradict the narrative, the shining city on the hill?

The wealthy make the history books, likewise the influential,
Their servants not considered consequential.
But the people long remember all the cruelties done unto them,
And sometimes the result is Revolution.

The trafficking in children peaked in sixteen ninety nine,
With a final flurry later on in seventeen nineteen.
But slavery takes many forms throughout the course of time.
Every generation has its variation on the theme.

In those days, British prisons were for those awaiting trial,
And they were overcrowded, rank, and vile.
And if you were convicted of a somewhat lesser crime,
You might be whipped, or branded, or be fined.

But for countless other crimes, including many forms of theft,
The only lawful punishment was death,
Until the Transportation Act of seventeen eighteen.
Convicts now could be transported overseas,

"For the use of any person," in other words, a slave,
For seven years, or fourteen years, no matter what their age.
And though children still were kidnapped by slave traders,
They were now the lesser source of forced white labor.

Shipping convicts to America was never well received.
We wanted honest laborers, not murderers and thieves.
But Britain sent their felons; some were idle, some were evil.
We viewed them as "the outcast of the people."

As time went on, the merchants found less profit to be made.
Our Declaration makes no reference to the convict transport trade.
In the "long train of abuses" is another form of slavery,
Impressment of our sailors by the British Royal Navy. [737]

LXX.

The drafting of soldiers to fight for the king,
And impressment of sailors to do the same thing,
Was a practice that dated to medieval times.
They could take almost anyone they happened to find.

The press gangs, in cutters, their small rapid boats,
Patrolling the harbors, and searching the coast,
Would raid all the taverns where sailors were drunk,
Or capture deserters before they could run.

In exchange for their traveling expenses and fees,
Armed bands of ruffians searched houses and streets,
Hauled grooms from their weddings, away from their brides,
And folk songs arose from the tears that were cried.

The gangs were most active upon the high seas.
They would board merchant vessels while armed to the teeth,
Taking most of the sailors to fight in the wars,
Leaving too small a crew to sail safely to shore.

The surrender at Yorktown did not end the curse.
Impressment of sailors grew many times worse,
Our ships were intercepted at every good chance,
For the king needed soldiers to fight against France.

The British impressed more than nine thousand men,
And we had to defeat them all over again.
In eighteen and twelve we declared a new war,
Once and for all to be rid of King George.

Our sailors were free now to plough the salt waves,
While the census recorded one million black slaves.
Their freedom would come at a terrible cost,
In treasure expended, and lives that were lost. [744]

LXXI.

Never underestimate the power of denial.
No matter what historical revisionists might say,
The cause of the Civil War was slavery.
There was no doubt among the leaders of the day.

No less an authority than Alexander Stephens,
Confederate Vice President, did say, and this is proven,
That slavery was the cause of both secession and rebellion,
Which he called the "rupture" and the "revolution."

The "corner stone" upon which the Confederacy rested
Was that Negroes are not equal to the white men,
That slavery was normal, and their natural condition.
These are Stephens' words, and we should cite them.

Revisionists can say the war was all about states' rights,
And I suppose it was, if that is how you frame it.
Keeping Africans in bondage was the "right" that mattered most.
'Tis a plain and simple truth, we must reclaim it.

There were other rivalries, not to be forgotten.
The North had all the industry, the South had all the cotton.
The North exploited workers while the South exploited slaves,
And the North imposed a tariff to protect the goods they made.

They say it was a rich man's war that poor men had to fight.
This is true of every war, and does not make it right.
Slavery was more widespread than many people say.
Many Southern households, one in three, owned Negro slaves.

Every rebel soldier had some reasons of his own,
Not the least of which was where the fighting happened.
The slave states were invaded by the armies of the North,
Except in Pennsylvania, and in Kansas.

We can honor fallen soldiers without honoring their cause.
It is altogether proper we should do this.
But remember that when some still hoped the war could be avoided,
The rebels fired first, and put us through this.

When Lincoln took the oath of office he repeated once again,
That because he had no legal right to do so,
He promised not to interfere where slavery existed.
He had said these words before; the people knew so.

The dispute was whether slavery should ever be extended
To the territories soon to join the Union.
Whether Congress had the power to prohibit or allow it
Was not resolved within the Constitution.

But if slavery could be confined to states where it existed,
One could hope for its eventual extinction,
For as new states joined the Union, the South would be outvoted.
This was the stated policy of Lincoln.

Freedom could be gradual, the owners compensated,
And a bloody war avoided in that way.
But we went to war instead, with six hundred thousand dead,
And the cost was twice the price of all the slaves.

Lincoln always hated slavery, he said so all along,
"A monstrous injustice," "moral evil."
"As I would not be a slave, so I would not be a master."
He believed "that all men are created equal."

It is true that Lincoln stated, once the Civil War began,
That his main objective was to save the Union.
But it was he who freed the slaves by Proclamation,
And a new amendment to the Constitution.

"Neither slavery nor involuntary servitude"
Would be allowed within our nation any more.
We still remembered both the sailors and the children,
Taken captive not so many years before.

The second time he took the oath of office,
He said what everyone had always known before,
He had accepted war, so the nation would not perish,
But slavery was "the cause of the war." [760]

LXXII.

In the year of eighteen eighty six a great adventure story
By Robert Louis Stevenson was published,
About a kidnap victim to be sold for the plantations,
The last time a great writer broached the subject.

An orphan boy in Scotland was the heir to an estate,
And his wicked uncle wished to disinherit him.
He brought him to the docks, for to watch the sailing ships,
And he climbed aboard, and out to sea they carried him.

He was bound for Carolina, and not merely as an exile.
The captain meant to sell him into slavery.
This happens in the year of seventeen and fifty one.
The book is fiction, but makes clear such things were done.

White men still were sold as slaves on the plantations.
The trade was much suppressed, but not unknown.
Many a man was forced to hoe tobacco overseas,
Who should have been upon his horse at home.

In the book, the ship is wrecked upon a reef,
And the boy is washed ashore upon an island.
With a famous Scottish rebel as his traveling companion,
He walks two hundred miles across the highlands.

In the year of nineteen thirty eight, a feature film was made,
Changing both the book and history beyond all recognition,
Adding a romantic plot to show off their new starlet.
Worse than this were the deliberate omissions.

The scenes that made us love the book are missing from the film:
The siege on board the sailing ship, the dangers in the wild.
And a single piece of candy lures the boy on board the ship.
They never say the purpose was enslavement of the child.

They were bound by a "production code" that governed motion pictures.
It was rigidly enforced, and certain things were never shown.
The explicit words "white slavery" were high upon the list,
With no further explanation as to what was meant by this.

Very likely, what they meant was prostitution.
But films were also not allowed to criticize
Another country's history or public institutions.
Their silence had the same effect as lies. [769]

LXXIII.

Two years ago, on the very same day,
Almost as if in collusion,
Two of America's media giants,
Sowing the seeds of confusion,

Both published statements "debunking a myth"
That the Irish had ever been slaves.
Calling the story "misleading" and "dangerous,"
These are the reasons they gave.

They "trace back" the story to "self-published books"
And to "white supremacist news sites, "
Blaming "neo-Confederates," "Nazis" and "racists"
For bringing this "false claim" to light.

They pick out a "meme" that is frequently referenced,
Copied and pasted, unedited,
Replete with wild numbers that cannot be true,
And are easily, therefore, discredited.

They troll social media, looking for photos,
Posted by users, as mere illustrations,
Stating the obvious, these were not taken
At times of forced Irish migration.

They deny Irish people were ever enslaved
After Cromwell's invasion of Ireland.
But the books of the Council of State say it happened,
Naming the ships and the captains.

Two thousand children, all fourteen or younger,
Were sent to Jamaica, and half of them girls.
To Virginia and Boston went four hundred more,
As if they were prisoners, taken at war.

Denying the story, they say it conflates
Indentured servants with African slaves.
The one had a contract, the other did not.
The one was for hire, the other was bought.

Indentured servitude lasted for years,
After which they became independent.
African slavery lasted for life,
And their status passed on to descendants.

And while these distinctions are true,
What they will never tell you,
Is that thousands of children were transported here
Without indentures, as my books make clear.

These kids were transported against their own will,
And there was no contract for them to fulfill.
They had hope of freedom, and kept their own names,
But during their bondage were slaves all the same.

'Tis a time honored tactic when hiding the truth,
To read what is written, and then pick and choose,
Refuting whatever can be proven wrong,
Ignoring the works that are solid and strong.

And who are the ones who denied this occurred,
On the very same day, in such similar words?
"The newspaper of record," the famed New York Times,
And our own public radio, called "P. R. I."

And don't get me wrong, I admire them both.
Their reporting, I find, is far better than most.
But this time they passed a false narrative on,
And they will not admit they were wrong. [783]

LXXIV.

There was a time when the people were told
How children were kidnapped, transported, and sold.
It was all written down in the history books.
Go to the library, have a good look.

Read Edward Channing, a Harvard professor,
Whose history, published in nineteen o eight,
Tells how white "servants" were treated as slaves,
And performed the hard labor in earlier days,

When Charles the Second was king, and long after,
When streets were infested with frightful kidnappers,
And most of their victims were young boys and girls,
Sent from London and Bristol unto the new world,

To Barbados, Jamaica, Virginia, and Maryland,
"Spirits" would take them, and slave ships would carry them,
Hundreds of ill-fated souls every year,
And the author reveals where the records appear.

James Truslow Adams, nineteen thirty two,
Begins with the story that all of us knew,
How those of good standing might find it attractive
To work a few years for to pay for their passage,

With not much to lose, and a sense of adventure,
They would quite willingly sign an indenture.
But "**wicked ships' captains**" moved in on the trade,
And kidnapped young children to sell them as slaves.

Or read Leo Huberman, writing for children.
His book, "We the People," nineteen thirty two,
Tells how the "spirited" servants were treated,
In plain, simple language that always rings true.

"The master might whip them whenever he liked,"
Or brand any servant who ran away twice,
Or dress them in rags, with no shelter or shade.
They were, while in service, "no better than slaves."

And when they were free, facing life on their own,
With some corn, a few tools, and a new suit of clothes,
Most of them left for the back country hills.
"Poor whites" and "hill-billies" are living there still.

Or read V. F. Calverton, easy to find.
He published his book in nineteen thirty nine.
Black and white slavery, here in our nation
Differed mainly, he said, "in regard to duration."

Only the blacks were in bondage for life,
But all were mere property, both black and white.
All were expected to serve out their time
If their master should sell them, or if he should die.

And if not enough white volunteers could be found,
The captains and companies prowled through the town,
Luring young children to holds of the ships,
Kidnapping them outright if it came to this.

Or read Samuel Eliot Morison's history,
Published at Oxford, nineteen sixty five.
He tells of "respectable" true volunteers.
To begin a new life, they would serve a few years.

"Next below these" were the rebels and prisoners,
Scottish and Irish, transported away,
Banished by Cromwell and all Stuart kings,
To West Indies, New England, and Chesapeake Bay.

He tells of the "crooks," the kidnappers in London,
And young boys and girls who were shipped overseas.
On arrival the captain would sell them to cover
The cost of the transport and kidnapper's fees.

These were historians, trusted and true.
Three were awarded the Pulitzer prize.
I discovered myself what they already knew,
In the records I saw with my very own eyes.

When you are done reading, do ask yourself how
It happens that we are not told of this now,
And why the truth tellers are so demonized.
Denial of truth is the same thing as lies. [800]

LXXV.

My song is over now, the tales are told.
A light is cast upon the days of old.
Revealing what in far too many ways
Had truly been a dark and dreadful age.

To anyone inclined to take offense,
I say to you, this is not my intent.
I only mean to tell the honest truth,
And honor those who suffered in their youth.

I do not mean to slight the Negro slaves
Who gained their freedom only in their graves,
Whose numbers were far greater than the whites.
But lesser wrongs do not equate to rights.

Slavery did not start out the same
As the racial institution it became.
History should never be erased.
Far better that the truth be squarely faced.

There is a ruling class, there always was,
Exploiting all the rest, it always does.
They did this to us all, both black and white.
We can remain divided, or unite.

And we must know what happened to us then
To understand what happens to us now.
And we should question why, and how, and when
Our knowledge of the past was disallowed.

In Scotland, ancient memories are clear.
Though it has been three hundred fifty years,
They still can name the ship, the Ewe and Lamb,
And both the skipper and the business man

Who kidnapped children at the Port of Leith,
And shipped them all across the raging sea.
The records of York County vouch for this.
A kidnapped boy identified the ship.

But we've forgotten now what we once knew.
Our narrative is not entirely true –
That only certain groups have been oppressed,
With "privilege" enjoyed by all the rest.

A careful look at history will show
That we have more in common than we know.
The workers of the world have always faced
Divisions more of class than those of race.

There are some of every color, every age,
Who work, but are not paid a living wage,
Who struggle to fulfill their basic needs,
While others have no limit to their greed.

When children are abused as much today,
Our institutions look the other way,
Or actively engage in what is done,
For there is nothing new under the sun.

'Twas ever thus, but need not always be.
We cannot change what we refuse to see.
What shall we leave to all our boys and girls?
'Tis not too late to seek a newer world. [813]

ANNOTATIONS

PART ONE

II. [verse 9] Rev. John Pike recorded the death of David Hamilton (sic) at the hands of Indians on 28 September 1692. (ref. Cutter, William Richard, Editor, "New England Families: Genealogical and Memorial," Volume IV, Clearfield Company, 1913, p. 1684). See historical marker on Sligo Road near Dover, New Hampshire.

II. [verse 10] David named one of his sons Gabriel, a name belonging exclusively to the Westburn branch if the Hambletons. (ref. Rev. Arthur Wentworth Hamilton Eaton, in "The New England Historical and Genealogical Register," Volume XLIV, New England Historic Genealogical Society, Boston, Mass., 1890, p. 361). He was probably the son of Andrew of Westburn, born 1548. (ref. Libby and Davis, "Genealogical Dictionary of Maine and New Hampshire," Genealogical Publishing Company, Baltimore, Maryland, 1972, p. 303).

II. [verse 11] "This family for centuries has been one of the most distinguished in Scotland and England, and closely related to royalty in both countries." (ref. Cutter, op cit., p. 1683). David Hambleton's direct ancestor was Mary Stewart, Princess of Scotland, daughter of James II of Scotland.

II. [verse 12] The birth dates of David Hambleton and Annah Jaxson are unknown. She is believed to have been as much as twenty years his junior.

II. [verse 13] "He was taken prisoner by Cromwell at the Battle of Worcester," 3 September 1651 (ref. Cutter, op cit., p. 1684), "brought to America as a prisoner in chains" aboard the *John and Sarah* (ref. historical marker, op cit.). His name appears on the passenger list (ref. Carl Boyer III, "Ship Passenger Lists: National and New England (1600-1825)," self-published, 1977, p. 155, citing "Scotch Prisoners Sent to Massachusetts in 1652, by Order of the English Government," in "The New England Historical and Genealogical Register, 1847, p. 377-380). He was "sold into slavery" (ref. Cutter, op cit., p. 1684) at Berwick, Maine, the going rate for healthy Scottish slave being about £30 (ref. Boyer, op cit., citing Charles Edward Banks, "Scotch Prisoners Deported to New England by Cromwell, 1651-52," Massachusetts Historical Society Proceedings, 61, 1928, pp. 4-29).

II. [verse 14] Deed from James Grant to David Hambleton, 7 October 1669, recorded in Rockingham County, New Hampshire, Deed Book 3, Page 94B.

II. [verse 15] Annah Jaxson married David Hambleton at Saco, Maine on 14 July 1662 (ref. "History of Saco and Biddeford," by George Folsom, printed by Alex. C. Putnam, Saco, Maine, 1830).

II. [verse 16] Deed from the Selectmen of the Town of Dover to Thomas Potts, 28 March 1698, recorded in Rockingham County, New Hampshire, Deed Book 7, Page 380.

II. [verse 17] "James Hamelton (sic) servant to James Bourn is adjudged to be twelve years of age and is ordered to serve according to law." (ref. Westmoreland County, Virginia, Order Book 1698-1699, 26 April 1699, p. 34a). Eaton (1890, op cit.) believes that James Hambleton was born in 1682.

II. [verse 18] "James Hambleton, servant to James Bourn, for his arrogant and sawcy words and behavior before this Court is ordered twenty lashes on his bare back well laid by the Sheriff," and "James Bourn complaining to this Court that his servant James Hambleton did violently assault him on the Queen's Road and the same being sufficiently prove, it is ordered that James Hambleton do serve his master one whole year after all former tyme of service by custome, indenture, order of Court or otherwise be fully expired." (ref. Westmoreland County, Virginia, Order Book, 26 March 1707, p. 45a).

II. [verse 19] Freed by Westmoreland County Court, 24 February 1714.

II. [verse 20] Deed from Henry Asbury Jr. to James Hambleton, 21 July 1725, Westmoreland County, Virginia, Deeds and Wills, Book 8, Page 53a. Last Will and Testament of James Hambleton, dated 17 November 1726, recorded 15 April 1727, and of Grace Hambleton, dated 11 February 1727, recorded 18 April 1727, Westmoreland County, Virginia, Deeds and Wills, Book 8, Pages 80 and 80a.

II. [verse 21] The old stone foundation, 32 feet by 24 feet, is on the west side of Sligo Road, just south of the intersection with Pinch Hill Road, very near the historical marker to David Hambleton and Annah Jaxson.

III. [verses 23-25] Richard Hayes Phillips, *"Without Indentures: Index to White Slave Children in Colonial Court Records,"* p. xi, citing Egerton Mss. 2395, folios 227-229, dated 1659, confirmed by Dr. Justin Clegg at British Museum.

III. [verses 27-28] *"Without Indentures,"* op. cit., pp. ix-xi, citing William Waller Hening, *"Statutes at Large; Virginia,"* March 1642-3, Act XXVI, March 1654-5, Act VI, March 1661-2, Act XCVIII, and *"Proceedings and Acts of the General Assembly; Maryland,"* Volume 1, October 1654, p. 352, April-May 1661, p. 409, April 1662, p. 453, and Volume 2, October 1671, p. 335.

IV. [verse 29] Westmoreland County, Virginia, Order Book 1698-1699, 26 April 1699.

IV. [verse 30] *"Without Indentures,"* op. cit., pp. 117-124. Altogether, the names of 305 children sentenced to terms of servitude ranging from five to twenty-one year are found in the Order Books of Westmoreland County, Virginia, 1663-1664, 1676-1723. The records for twelve years have been lost, owing to the ravages of time.

IV. [verse 34] Sometimes, tucked between the pages, were notes and receipts which had yellowed the pages in precisely the same positions as I found them, thus proving that nobody had looked at those books for centuries. My hands tingled as I touched them. (ref. *"Without Indentures,"* op. cit., p. xvii). An archivist at the Hall of Records in Annapolis, Maryland said to me, without exaggeration: "Nobody looks at these."

IV. [verse 34] Altogether, the names of 5290 children sentenced to terms of servitude are listed in *"Without Indentures,"* op. cit., and another 38 in Richard Hayes Phillips, *"White Slave Children of Colonial Maryland and Virginia: Birth and Shipping Records,"* pp. 369-370.

V. [verse 36] The surnames of these white slave children are paired with the names of the "Worshippfull Commissioners" and "Gentlemen Justices" who owned them, county by county, in *"Without Indentures,"* op. cit.

V. [verse 39] Altogether, 677 children sentenced to terms of servitude in 1699 are listed in *"Without Indentures,"* op. cit., and another six in *"Birth and Shipping Records,"* op. cit., pp. 370, 372. Two more, one in Bucks County, Pennsylvania, and one in Burlington County, New Jersey, are listed in this book. The next highest totals are 235 in 1698, and 204 in 1700 (plus one in 1698 and four in 1700, found in Kent County, Delaware, listed in *"Birth and Shipping Records,"* op. cit., p. 372). The annual breakdown is presented in *"Without Indentures,"* op. cit., p. xiii.

V . [verse 40] The annual breakdown of imported Negro children sentenced to slavery is presented in *"Without Indentures,"* op. cit., p. xiv.

V. [verse 42] If the children identified the ships that transported them and/or the captains who commanded those ships, the exact wording from the court records is abstracted in the indexes of *"Without Indentures,"* op. cit. The judges in most counties never asked the question. All but 20 of the 460 children who identified the ships and/or the captains were in York, Middlesex, Surry or Essex Counties, Virginia, or Somerset County, Maryland.

VI. [verse 47] The sources for Bristol shipping records are identified in *"Birth and Shipping Records,"* op. cit., p. 336, entries 3, 6, 7, 8.

VI. [verse 51] The source for Boston shipping records is identified in *"Birth and Shipping Records,"* op. cit., p. 337, entry 2.

VI. [verse 51] The source for Scotland shipping records is identified in *"Birth and Shipping Records,"* op. cit., p. 338, entry 2.

VII. [verse 55] Griffin, Grace Gardner, *"A Guide to Manuscripts Relating to American History in British Depositories,"* Reproduced for the Division of Manuscripts of the Library of Congress (Washington, D.C., 1946).

VII. [verse 56] Public Record Office, London, Colonial Office 5, Vol. 749. Shipping returns, Maryland. 1689-1702. Complete. Photostats. 282 prints in 5 parts, 447 equivalent pages. Received by Library of Congress February 7, 1939. Cited by Griffin, *"Guide to Manuscripts,"* op. cit.

VII. [verse 57] It took me two days just to photograph them.

VII. [verse 61] ref. "Duties Paid for Imported White Servants," in *"Birth and Shipping Records,"* op. cit., pp. 339-343.

VII. [verse 62] ref. "Kids as Cargo," in *"Birth and Shipping Records,"* op. cit., pp. 10-14.

VII. [verse 63] At least 907 were transported in 1698. ref. "Duties Paid for Imported White Servants," in *"Birth and Shipping Records,"* op. cit., pp. 340-343.

VII. [verses 64-66] The movements of 170 white slave ships are tracked in *"Birth and Shipping Records,"* op. cit., pp. 300-335.

VII. [verse 71] Many eastern Virginia counties suffered catastrophic losses of their early records due to military activity, predominantly during the Civil War, when most or all of the court records for Charles City County, James City County, Stafford County, and Warwick County, among others, were lost. (ref. https://www.lva.virginia.gov/public/guides/rn30_lostrecords.pdf) One of the reasons why the early records in so many Chesapeake counties have survived is because they are located on peninsulas, where military troops would not have ventured for fear of being trapped.

VIII. [verses 72-83]

"All Irish genealogical records were destroyed in the 1922 fire: Myth or fact?" ref. https://www.irish-genealogy-toolkit.com/irish-records-burned.html

"Battle of Dublin," ref. https://en.wikipedia.org/wiki/Battle_of_Dublin

"The Bombardment of the Four Courts and the beginning of the Irish Civil War, 28 June 1922," by Bruce Gaston, ref. https://www.irishhistorycompressed.com/the-bombardment-of-the-four-courts-28-june-1922

"British Military Involvement in the Irish Civil War," by John Dorney, ref. http://www.theirishstory.com/2012/11/25/british-military-involvement-in-the-irish-civil-war/#.XOqvdHdFyM8

"The Irish Civil War – A brief overview," by John Dorney, ref. http://www.theirishstory.com/2012/07/02/the-irish-civil-war-a-brief-overview/#.XOqubXdFyM8

"Ruin of Public Record Office marked loss of great archive," by Caitriona Crowe, ref. https://www.irishtimes.com/opinion/ruin-of-public-record-office-marked-loss-of-great-archive-1.1069843

IX. [verse 85] The surviving parish registers dating to seventeenth century Ireland are available as follows. Cork, Derry and Dublin: transcribed and published by Representative Church Body Library (Dublin), or William Pollard & Co., Ltd. (Exeter and London), or Alex. Thom & Co. Ltd. (Dublin); abstracted in *"Birth and Shipping Records,"* op. cit., pp. 231-241. Lisburn, southwest of Belfast: on microfilm at Public Records Office of Northern Ireland (PRONI); abstract included in this book, having been omitted by mistake from *"Birth and Shipping Records,"* op. cit.

IX. [verses 86-87] Surviving town records or parish registers are available online as specified in *"Birth and Shipping Records,"* op. cit., pp. 59, 65, 78, 83, 111, 134, 136, 138, 191, 194, 199, 201, 203, 207, 253.

IX. [verse 88] Since the publication of *"Birth and Shipping Records,"* op. cit., I was informed by the London Metropolitan Archives that baptismal records from London, dating to the seventeenth century, have been published online:

"London, England, Church of England Baptisms, Marriages and Burials, 1538-1812," ref. https://www.ancestry.com/search/collections/lmaearlyparish

Also, the parish records from the shire of Essex, downriver from London, have been published online:

"*Essex, England, Church of England Baptisms, Marriages, and Burials, 1538-1912,*" ref. https://www.ancestry.com/search/collections/essexearlyparish

The records previously abstracted in "*Birth and Shipping Records,*" op. cit., have been updated accordingly, and are published in "*White Slave Children: Supplement to the Trilogy,*" pp. 6-32.

X. [verse 91] "*Whitehaven Walks, Maritime & Mining, Walk 3,*" by Anne Cook, Whitehaven Town Historian. Available at the Beacon Museum in Whitehaven.

X. [verse 92] John Hutton, son of James Hutton, baptized 28 July 1672, Wigton, Cumberland, England, was adjudged on 19 February 1679 to be 7 years of age and sentenced to 17 years in Northumberland County, Virginia.

X. [verse 92] "The iron cuffs are still upon the walls." Personal communication from a Council member, February 2015.

X. [verse 95] Potential escape routes are evident today. Upon reaching the beach at the bottom of the sea cliffs, there are plenty of places to hide from anyone viewing from above. Personal observation.

X. [verse 97] The *Ruby of White Haven* was identified by Thomas Sherwine on 10 August 1697 as having transported him to Somerset County, Maryland (ref. "*Without Indentures,*" op. cit., p. 28). The records for the other five ships, sailing from Whitehaven, listed "European goods and servants" as "Generall Cargo" in 1699, 1700, or 1701 (ref. "*Birth and Shipping Records,*" op. cit., pp. 12, 13, 14, 317, 319, 327, 328, 345, 347, 349).

X. [verse 98] Fourteen kids are identified as having been transported from Cumberland between 1697 and 1701. Of these, eight were boys adjudged to be under fourteen years of age (ref. "*Birth and Shipping Records,*" op. cit., pp. 59-64). Under English Common Law, it was not lawful for boys under fourteen years of age to select their own guardian, to serve as an apprentice, or to sign contracts, which would include indentures (ref. "Age of Consent," in "*Birth and Shipping Records,*" op. cit., p. xxix).

XI. [verse 101] ref. "*Without Indentures,*" op. cit., pp. 191-200, 205-223.

XI. [verse 102] ref. "Owners of White Slave Ships," in "*Birth and Shipping Records,*" op. cit., p. 351, citing Petition of Nathaniel Bacon, John Page, Thomas Thorp and George Poindexter, to Lord Culpeper, 19 November 1681, in "*Calendar of State Papers Colonial, America and West Indies, Vol. 11, 1681-1685,*" pp. 135 et seq.

XI. [verse 102] ref. "Profiles of Child Traffickers," in *"Birth and Shipping Records,"* op. cit., pp. 19, 27-28, 30.

XI. [verse 103] ref. "Profiles of Child Traffickers," in *"Birth and Shipping Records,"* op. cit., pp. 25-26.

XI. [verse 104] Duke of York, Royal Navy ship, first used for a Hired Ship in 1664, ref. *"Birth and Shipping Records,"* op. cit., p. 304, citing https://www.naval-history.net/xGM-Chrono-01BB-HMS_Duke_of_York.htm

XI. [verse 103] ref. Gentleman Justices, York County, Virginia, in *"Without Indentures,"* op. cit., pp. 224-227.

XI. [verse 104] ref. *"Without Indentures,"* op. cit., pp. 152-169, 191-200, 205-223.

XI. [verse 105] The four owners, by name, were Col. Cuthbert Potter, Major Genl. Robert Smith, Ralph Wormley Esq., Sir Henry Chicheley Lt. Gov. of Virginia (ref. "Owners of White Slave Ships," in *"Birth and Shipping Records,"* op. cit., p. 351, citing Hening, *"Statutes at Large; Virginia,"* op. cit., 1682-1710, pp. 543 et seq.)

XI. [verse 105] ref. Gentleman Justices, Middlesex County, Virginia, in *"Without Indentures,"* op. cit., pp. 201-203.

XI. [verse 105] Sir Henry Chicheley was twice the Acting Governor of Virginia (30 December 1678 – 10 May 1680, and 11 August 1680 – December 1682) during the mostly absentee administration of Sir Thomas Culpeper.

XI. [verse 106] ref. *"Without Indentures,"* op. cit., pp. 201-203, 224-227.

XI. [verse 107] ref. *"Birth and Shipping Records,"* op. cit., pp. 304, 312.

XI. [verse 108] ref. *"Birth and Shipping Records,"* op. cit., p. 320, and "Index to Ship Arrivals," in *"Without Indentures,"* op. cit., p. 253.

XI. [verse 109] ref. *"Without Indentures,"* op. cit., pp. 205-223.

XI. [verse 109] Sir Thomas Grantham, Commander of the *Concord of London*, a ship of 32 guns, was sent up the James River to put down Bacon's Rebellion on 21 November 1676. (The Court Records of York County, Virginia do not indicate that children were transported on this voyage). ref. Stephen Saunders Webb, *"1676: The End of American Independence,"* p. 111. See also https://en.wikisource.org/wiki/Grantham,_Thomas_(fl.1684)_(DNB00)

XI. [verse 110] ref. *"Birth and Shipping Records,"* op. cit., p. 320.

XII. [verse 111] For a concise accounting of three shipments of one hundred children each, with references, see *"Without Indentures,"* op. cit., pp. xi-xii.

XII. [verses 112-114] For the complete text of the Privy Council Order of 26 July 1660, see *"Without Indentures,"* op. cit., p. xvi, citing "Acts of the Privy Council of England, Colonial Series, Vol. I, 1613-1680," W. L. Grant, M.A., editor, published 1908, pages 296-297.

XII. [verses 115-117] ref. *"Birth and Shipping Records,"* op. cit., pp. 1-2.

XII. [verse 118] Compare "Duties Paid for Imported White Servants" (pp. 339-343) with "Duties Paid for Imported Negro Slaves" (pp. 352-354), in *"Birth and Shipping Records,"* op. cit.

XII. [verse 119] ref. *"Birth and Shipping Records,"* op. cit., pp. 354, 355.

XII. [verse 120] ref. "Negro and Indian Children Brought to Court," in *"Without Indentures,"* op. cit., p. xiv.

XII. [verse 121] ref. *"Without Indentures,"* op. cit., p. xxxii. See also http://www.lva.virginia.gov/public/guides/tithables_vanote.htm

XIII. [verse 124] On 29 April 1619, the Virginia Company reported that the ship *Diana*, having "left England with the one hundred children from London, hath arrived with about eighty." (ref. *"Without Indentures,"* op. cit., p. xii, citing Alexander Brown, *"The first republic in America,"* pages 307-308, images of full text at https://archive.org/details/firstrepublicina00browuoft This was four months prior to the arrival at Point Comfort of "20 and odd Negroes" on "a Dutch man of Warr" commanded by Captain Jope in "the latter end of August." (ref. *"Without Indentures,"* op. cit., p. xx, citing Letter from John Rolfe to Sir Edwin Sandys, January 1620, Ferrar Papers. Document in Magdalene College, Cambridge. List of Records No. 154, full transcript at http://xtf.lib.virginia.edu/xtf/view?docId=2005_Q3_2/uvaGenText/tei/b002 245360.xml;chunk.id=d103;toc.depth=1;toc.id=;brand=default

XIII. [verse 125] Such wording may be found in the documents cited in *"Without Indentures,"* op. cit., pp. xi-xii.

XIII. [verse 128] For the full list of 181 children, ref. "Kids from Devon," in *"Birth and Shipping Records,"* op. cit., pp. 111-133. For the full list of 37 children who had lost one or both parents, ref. "Devon Children with Deceased Parents," in *"Birth and Shipping Records,"* op. cit., p. 4.

XIII. [verse 128] For the full list of 181 children, ref. "Kids from Devon," in *"Birth and Shipping Records,"* op. cit., pp. 111-133. For the full list of 37 children who had lost one or both parents, ref. "Devon Children with Deceased Parents," in *"Birth and Shipping Records,"* op. cit., p. 4.

XIII. [verses 130-131] Compare the names of the fathers and the dates of the court appearances of their children (pp. 114, 119, 123) with the burial dates of the fathers (p. 4), in *"Birth and Shipping Records,"* op. cit.

XIII. [verses 132-133] ref. "Targeted Families," in *"Birth and Shipping Records,"* op. cit., p. 8.

XIII. [verse 134] Ralfe Thommes, a.k.a. Ralph Tombs, the elder, appears on two lists of "Plymouth subscribers for redemption of captives in Turkey and Algiers 1680." www.findmypast.co.uk His son, Ralph Toms, the younger, baptized 13 April 1662, was adjudged on 18 December 1676 to be 14 years of age and sentenced to 10 years in Accomack County, Virginia.

XIII. [verses 136-137] The burial record of John Buckley says "minister of this parish" (Wolborough, Saint Mary). The baptismal record of David Williams says "David the son of John Williams minister" (Plympton Erle). The burial record of Theophilus Powell says "Rector of this parish" (Langtree).

XIII. [verse 137] The Attorney General reported "there being scarce any voyage to the Plantations but some were carried away against their wills." ref. *"Without Indentures,"* op. cit., p. xvi, citing *"Calendar of State Papers Colonial, America and West Indies, Volume 5: 1661-1668,"* W. Noel Sainsbury (editor), published 1880, Preface, pages xxviii-xxix. Spiriting away people to the Plantations.

XIV. [verse 138] The *Duke of Yorke*, the *Providence of London*, and the *Rainbow of Plymouth* all sailed to Lancaster County, Virginia in 1664 (ref. "Index to Ship Arrivals," in *"Without Indentures,"* op. cit., pp. 253-256).

XIV. [verse 139] These ports of departure were in the very names of the ships: *Adventure of Biddeford*, *Fisher of Biddeford*, *Jonathan of Topsham*, *Rainbow of Plymouth*. All were identified in the court records of colonial Maryland or Virginia by children transported upon them.

XIV. [verse 140] ref. "Kids from Devon," in *"Birth and Shipping Records,"* op. cit., pp. 111-133.

XIV. [verses 141-142] *"Birth and Shipping Records,"* op. cit., pp. 4, 119.

XIV. [verse 146] *"Birth and Shipping Records,"* op. cit., p. 121.

XIV. [verses 147-149] S. Baring-Gould, *"The Book of the West, Volume I, Devon,"* Methuen & Co., London, and New Amsterdam Book Co., New York, 1900, pp. 158, 176; and Robert Burnard, "Introductory Article: Dartmoor Preservation," in *"The Western Antiquary, or Devon and Cornwall Note-book, Volume 9,"* Elliot Stock, London, and J. W. Bouton, New York, c. 1881, p. 5.

XIV. [verses 150-151] *"Birth and Shipping Records,"* op. cit., p. 112.

XIV. [verse 152] "The Song of the Moor," in *"The Book of the West,"* op. cit., pp. 206-207. See also S. Baring-Gould et al., *"Songs of the West: Folk Songs of Devon & Cornwall,"* Methuen & Co., London, c. 1900, pp. 148-149, online in its entirety at https://archive.org/details/SongsOfTheWest/page/n1

PART TWO

XV. [verse 154] ref. *"Without Indentures,"* op. cit., p. ix, citing Hening, *"Statutes at Large; Virginia,"* op. cit., March 1642-3, Act XXVI.

XV. [verse 155] ref. *"Without Indentures,"* op. cit., p. xiii, citing *"Calendar of State Papers Colonial, America and West Indies, Volume 1: 1574-1660,"* W. Noel Sainsbury (editor), published 1860, pages 407-409. 1653. Sept. 6. Order of the Council of State.

XV. [verse 156] ref. *"Without Indentures,"* op. cit., pp. ix-x, citing Hening, *"Statutes at Large; Virginia,"* op. cit., March 1654-5, Act VI.

XV. [verse 157] ref. *"Without Indentures,"* op. cit., p. xi, citing Egerton Mss. 2395, folios 227-229, dated 1659, confirmed by Dr. Justin Clegg at British Museum.

XV. [verse 157] Altogether, at least 5328 children without indentures were ordered into servitude by the courts of colonial Maryland and Virginia. Not once were any of them asked how they came to be on board the ship in the first place. Only one, John Lyme, was allowed to make such a statement on the record, at County Court in Somerset County, Maryland, 15 January 1690: "Your poor petitioner was spirited out of his native country, unknown to any of his friends, and shipped aboard for this country as a servant." (ref. *"Without Indentures,"* op. cit., p. 1).

XV. [verse 158] The annual breakdown is presented in *"Without Indentures,"* op. cit., p. xiii.

XV. [verse 159] These eight children who were sentenced in 1660 appear in the indexes of *"Birth and Shipping Records,"* op. cit. – Henry Ellis, Gloucester (p. 90); John Hitchcox, Gloucester (p. 93); George Abbott, London (p. 138); Richard Curtis, London (p. 148); David Evans, London (p. 153); William Gant, Newcastle (p. 204); William Hood, Newcastle (p. 204); William Owens, Edinburgh (p. 224). In addition, there were two children identified as Irish whose birth records cannot be found (p. 266).

XV. [verse 160] ref. *"Without Indentures,"* op. cit., p. x, citing Hening, *"Statutes at Large; Virginia,"* op. cit., March 1661-2, Act XCVIII.

XV. [verse 161] ref. *"Without Indentures,"* op. cit., p. xi, citing *"Proceedings and Acts of the General Assembly,"* April 1666-June 1676, Volume 2, Page 335, October 1671. Those under fifteen were to serve until the age of twenty-two.

XVI. [verse 164] *"Birth and Shipping Records,"* op. cit., p. 168.

XVI. [verses 165-166] ref. *"Without Indentures,"* op. cit., p. vii.

XVI. [verse 166] John Lyme's adjudged age was not entered into the court record, but he was sentenced to seven years, which, according to Maryland law, fixes his adjudged age bracket as fifteen to eighteen years.

XVI. [verses 167-169] Richard Hayes Phillips, *"White Slave Children of Charles County, Maryland: The Search for Survivors,"* p. 33, citing Charles County Court Records, 1658-1694, 1696-1734, Maryland State Archives Volumes MSA CM376-1 to MSA CM376-32., 10 June 1690 [17.pdf #18].

Citations in *"The Search for Survivors"* refer to the .pdf file numbers and image numbers on the website of the Maryland State Archives.

XVI. [verse 170] *"The Search for Survivors,"* op. cit., p. 33, citing Charles County Court Records, 12 January 1686 [13.pdf #47], 9 February 1686 [13.pdf #48], 9 March 1686 [13.pdf #49]. The judges, by name, were Henry Hawkins Jr. and John Court Jr., both of whom were on the bench in Charles County Court on 10 June 1690, the day the "Kidnappers Indentures" were ruled invalid. [17.pdf #18]

XVI. [verse 172] *"The Search for Survivors,"* op. cit., p. 33, citing Charles County Court Records, 10 June 1690 [17.pdf #18].

XVI. [verse 172] Because the "Kidnappers Indentures" were for terms of four years, we know that the ship commanded by John Bowman had left Gravesend four years earlier, in 1686. John Lyme appeared in Somerset County Court on 15 January 1690, having arrived four years earlier, in 1686 (ref. *"Without Indentures,"* op. cit., pp. vii, 26).

XVII. [verse 175] The story of Thomas Waughop (a.k.a. Walkup) appears in *"Birth and Shipping Records,"* op. cit., p. vii.

XVII. [verse 177] ref. *"Without Indentures,"* op. cit., p. 145. Adjudged to be nine years of age, he would, under Virginia law, serve until the age of 24.

XVII. [verses 178-179] ref. *"Birth and Shipping Records,"* op. cit., p. 262.

XVIII. [verses 183-187] See "Index to Orphans," in *"The Search for Survivors,"* op. cit., pp. 351-391.

XVIII. [verse 183] The requirements that orphans were to have proper washing, lodging and clothing was routinely stated in the Court records.

XVIII. [verse 183] Orphans taught to read, without attending school: John Griggs, p. 364; Ralph Gwinn, p. 364; John Lange, p. 372; Robert Lange, p. 372; William Lange, p. 372; Elizabeth Sennet, p. 382; Jane Stigaleer, p. 385; Edward Williams, p. 390; in *"The Search for Survivors,"* op. cit.

XVIII. [verse 184] Orphans sent to school: Thomas Barron, p. 352; William Carpenter, p. 356; Joseph Dove, p. 360; Thomas Ford, p. 362; William Gray, p. 364; George Griggs, p. 364; Ralph Hedges, p. 366; Richard Higgins, p. 367; Ignatius Jennians, p. 369; William Jones, p. 370; John Pattison, p. 377; John Payne, p. 377; Penelope Perry, p. 378; Anne Richardson, p. 379; Joseph Richardson, p. 379; John Scroggin, pp. 381-382; Ralph Skidmore, p. 383; John Stanfield, p. 385; Hannah Weavour, p. 388; William Wharton, p. 388; Thomas Williams, p. 390; in *"The Search for Survivors,"* op. cit.

XVIII. [verse 185] Orphans taught a trade, many of whom were given tools: Thomas Barron, p. 352; Francis Capshaw, p. 355; John Capshaw, p. 355; John Carver, p. 356; Richard Carver, p. 356; John Cherrybub, p. 356; Jeremiah Dickason, p. 360; Thomas Douglass, p. 360; John Doy, p. 360; Nimrod Dunkin, p. 361; Thomas Ford, p. 362; Charles Garrett, p. 363; Richard Harrison, p. 366; Edward Hickson, p. 366; James Hickson, p. 367; Richard Higgins, p. 367; Giles Hill, p. 367; John Hill, p. 368; Richard Jones, p. 370; Edward Kite, p. 371; John Lange, p. 372; James Mankin, p. 373; James Murphey, p. 376; John Murphey, p. 376; Jonathan Nichols, p. 376; John Penn, p. 377; Marke Penn, p. 377-378;

Richard Price, p. 379; Charles Regon, p. 379; Elias Scarry, p. 380; Richard Scarry, p. 381; Nicholas Skidmore, p. 382; Ralph Skidmore, pp. 382-383; Edward Smoote, p. 384; Leonard Smoot, p. 384; John Stewart, p. 385; Adam Weavour, p. 388; George Witter, p. 391; Willam Witter, p. 391; in *"The Search for Survivors,"* op. cit.

XVIII. [verse 186] The requirements for decent clothing at the end of a term of service were universal, applying not only to apprenticed orphans, but also to servants with or without indentures. ref. "Perpetual Laws of Maryland," Charles County Court Records, 1677 [12.pdf #170, Folio 91]. For examples see "Encyclopedia of Survivors" in *"The Search for Survivors,"* op. cit.: Hugh Davies, p. 103; Owen Doyne, p. 106; John Luccraft, p. 126; John Wilkinson, pp. 154-155; Edward Williams, pp. 156-157; in *"The Search for Survivors,"* op. cit.

XVIII. [verse 187] Orphans given horses or cows: Andrew Baker, p. 351; Mathew Boswell, p. 354; John Browne, p. 355; William Carpenter, p. 356; Robert Doughaley, p. 360; George Griggs, p. 364; Anne Grumbold, p. 364; Thomas Hedges, p. 366; Elizabeth Heyfeild, p. 366; Richard Higgins, p. 367; Thomas Howard, p. 368; William Jackson, p. 369; William Jones, p. 370; John Maning, p. 373; William Olavery, p. 377; John Payne, p. 377; William Perkins, p. 378; John Phipps, p. 378; Edward Scarry, p. 380; Richard Scarry, p. 381; John Scroggin, pp. 381-382; Marmaduke Semmes, p. 382; Ralph Skidmore, p. 383; William Smith, p. 384; Jane Sommers, p. 385; John Wallis, p. 387; Mary Whittford, p. 389; William Willson Junr., p. 390; Benjamin Wise, p. 391; in *"The Search for Survivors,"* op. cit.

XVIII. [verse 189] ref. *"Without Indentures,"* op. cit., p. xv, citing *"Proceedings and Acts of the General Assembly,"* January 1637/8-September 1664, op. cit., Volume 1, Page 496, Sept.-Oct. 1663.

XVIII. [verse 190] ref. *"Without Indentures,"* op. cit., p. xv, citing Hening, *"Statutes at Large; Virginia,"* op. cit., October 1705, Act XIII. Freedom dues.

XVIII. [verse 191] ref. *"Without Indentures,"* op. cit., p. xv, citing *"Proceedings and Acts of the General Assembly,"* January 1637/8-September 1664, op. cit., Volume 1, page 331, August 1651.

XIX. [verses 192-197] ref. *"The Search for Survivors,"* op. cit., pp. 28, 248, citing Charles County Court Records, 3 November 1663, pp. 192-194 [02.pdf #255, 256, 257].

XX. [verses 198-203] Map of Chesapeake Bay, 1671, at frontispiece. See also Nathaniel Mason Pawlett, *"A Brief History of the Roads of Virginia 1607-1840,"* Virginia Highway & Transportation Research Council, 1977, 2003, pp. 4-7, http://www.virginiadot.org/vtrc/main/online_reports/pdf/78-r16.pdf See also "Atlantic Seaboard fall line" on Wikipedia.

XXI. [verse 205] ref. *"Without Indentures,"* op. cit., p. xiv, citing Hening, *"Statutes at Large; Virginia,"* op. cit., March 1642-3, Act XXII.

XXI. [verse 205] ref. *"Without Indentures,"* op. cit., p. xv, citing "An Act Relating to Servants and Slaves," Charles County Court Record, 1684-1685, microfilm reel CR 35691-3, MSA CM376-12, images 169, 170, Hall of Records, Maryland State Archives, Annapolis, Maryland. [12.pdf #169, #170]

XXI. [verses 206-207] ref. *"The Search for Survivors,"* op. cit., pp. 42-45.

XXI. [verses 208-212] ref. *"The Search for Survivors,"* op. cit., p. 41.

XXII. [verse 213] ref. *"The Search for Survivors,"* op. cit., p. 39. Virginia law phrased it this way: "negroes who are incapable of makeing satisfaction by addition of time" (Hening, *"Statutes at Large; Virginia,"* op cit., March 1660/61, Act XXII).

XXII. [verse 214] ref. *"The Search for Survivors,"* op. cit., p. 39, citing Hening, *"Statutes at Large; Virginia,"* op cit., March 1660/61, Act I.

XXII. [verse 215] ref. *"The Search for Survivors,"* op. cit., p. 37. The Court considered the age of freedom for Mulattoes to be thirty-one, but the law actually stated the age of thirty. For the full text, see "An Act Concerning Negroes and other Slaves made Anno 1664" [12.pdf #140, Folio 24]

XXII. [verse 215] Orphan girls freed at the age of sixteen included: Francis Harmon, p. 365; Mary Manwaring, p. 374; Mary Roberts, p. 379; Elizabeth Typpett, p. 386; Mary Whittford, p. 389; and Sarah "a Molattoe girl," p. 232; in *"The Search for Survivors,"* op. cit.

XXII. [verse 215] Orphan boys freed at the age of twenty-one included: Nicholas Belaine, p. 353; Francis Crompton, p. 359; William Darby, p. 359; Jeremiah Dickason, p. 360; Richard Fowke, p. 362; Edward Gardainer, p. 363; Thomas Hedges, p. 366; John Maud, p. 375; Elias Scarry, p. 381; William Willson Junr., p. 390; and John Birke, "a Mollatto," p. 205; in *"The Search for Survivors,"* op. cit.

XXII. [verses 216-218] John Glover, pp. 36, 39, 179, 215, 259; Thomas Fountain, pp. 1, 25, 40, 178, 362; Mollatto Will, pp. 1, 28, 39, 190; in *"The Search for Survivors,"* op. cit.

XXIII. [verses 219-227] Rosamond Law, pp. 1, 29, 42, 185; Silent Ball, pp. 1, 43, 44, 48, 167; John Bacon, pp. 1, 26, 43, 166; in *"The Search for Survivors,"* op. cit.

XXIV. [verse 228] Elizabeth Hasellton does not appear on the list of children without indentures compiled from the Charles County Court Records (ref. *"Without Indentures,"* op. cit, pp. 84-107, revised in *"The Search for Survivors,"* op. cit., pp. 61-86). All the Court Records for this time period still exist.

XXIV. [verses 228-237] The story of Elizabeth Hasellton is presented in graphic detail in *"The Search for Survivors,"* op. cit., pp. 25, 243-244, citing Charles County Court Records, 11 January 1670, Archives of Maryland Online, Volume 60, Pages 233-235.

XXIV. [verse 229] ref. Charles County Court Records, 12 March 1666/7 (sixteen days), 11 June 1667 (twelve days), and 13 August 1667 (ten days). In these earliest records her name is presented as Hasellton or Haselton.

XXIV. [verse 235] Anne Lane, servant to Humphery Warren, was brought to Charles County Court on 17 March 1663 and adjudged to be eighteen years of age (born c. 1645). A targeted search of birth and baptismal records finds her as Ann Layne, daughter of Richard and Ann Layne, baptized 8 September 1644, Saint Bride **Fleet Street**, London, England (ref. "Kids from London," in *"Birth and Shipping Records,"* op. cit., p. 166; and "Encyclopedia of Survivors," in *"The Search for Survivors,"* op. cit., p.125. Her expected date of freedom would have been 1670. The Charles County Court Record for 11 January 1670 identifies her as "Anne Lane aged 25 yeares or thereabouts."

XXV. [verses 238-242] The story of Abigail Clampett is presented in graphic detail in *"The Search for Survivors,"* op. cit., pp. 27, 241-242, citing Charles County Court Records, 9 November 1703 [22.pdf #144].

XXVI. [verses 243-251] ref. *"The Search for Survivors,"* op. cit., pp. vii-viii, 111. John Green told his own story, which was written in the Charles County Court Records, 14 November 1676 [07.pdf #129].

XXVI. [verse 244] Benjamin Rozer is first identified as "high Sherrife" of Charles County on 10 September 1667, Archives of Maryland Online, Volume 60, Page 106.

XXVI. [verse 244] Daniell Johnson held eight deeds to real estate in Charles County, including seven patents from the Province of Maryland, dated 1661 to 1663, for 750 acres, 200 acres, 200 acres, 700 acres, 100 acres, 300 acres, and 100 acres, or 2350 acres altogether (ref. "Grantee Index to Deeds," in *"The Search for Survivors,"* p. 306).

XXVI. [verse 245] Daniell Johnson first appears in the Charles County Court Records as deceased on 10 March 1671. His widow Elizabeth Johnson is named as Administratrix [06.pdf #39]. A scant three months later, on 13 June 1671 John and Elizabeth Kilborne are both named as administrators of the estate of Daniell Johnson [06.pdf #46].

XXVI. [verse 247] ref. *"The Search for Survivors,"* op. cit., p. viii. It was not lawful for any master to make any bargain with any servant for any time longer, "not untill his first time of servitude be fully expired." There were six subsequent petitions for freedom that succeeded on this basis: Margarett Atkinson, 13 January 1680 [09.pdf #152]; Grace Holmes, 13 March 1694 [18.pdf #145]; George Carter, 9 March 1708 [23.pdf #237]; Francis Ross, 13 June 1710 [23.pdf #402]; William Hilton, 10 August 1714 [25.pdf #243]; and Joan Ruby, 14 March 1721 [27.pdf 45].

XXVI. [verse 249] ref. Mount Vernon VA (1888) and Patuxent MD (1897) USGS 30 minute topographic maps (1:125.000), showing Piscataway Creek, Port Tobacco, and the terrain in between.

XXVII. [verse 252] Phillipe Lynes, son of Henry and Mary Lynes, Baptized 17 November 1646, Saint Andrew, Holborn, Camden, London, England.

XXVII. [verse 252] Between 1676 and 1693, Philip Lynes purchased twenty-eight servants without indentures, two of them (John Greene and Elizabeth Maybanck) from their previous masters, and at least twenty-one indentured servants. Almost certainly, there were more. Indentured servants did not appear before the court to have their ages adjudged, because there was a written contract consigning them to servitude. The only indentured servants appearing on the record were the recaptured runaways (there were twelve), those petitioning for freedom (there were nineteen), or those complaining of abuse or neglect (there were nine). Most of them fell into more than one of these categories. No other master had so many complaints.

XXVII. [verse 252] Philip Lynes held thirty-four deeds to real estate in Charles County, thirty-one of them dated 1674 to 1690, the other three dated 1706 or 1707. By 1680 he had purchased nearly 4000 acres of land. By 1690 he had purchased more than 7000 acres, about eleven square miles (ref. "Grantee Index to Deeds," in *"The Search for Survivors,"* op. cit., pp. 308-309).

XXVII. [verse 253] On 13 June 1676, Philip Lines "Gentleman," probably twenty-nine years old, was sworn as an attorney of the Charles County Court. ref. *"The Search for Survivors,"* op. cit., p. 6, citing [07.pdf #111].

XXVII. [verses 254-255] A transcript of the Charles County Court Record concerning Philip Lynes' assault upon Thomas Smith, 9 March 1680, is presented in *"The Search for Survivors,"* op. cit., p. 6, citing [09.pdf #154].

XXVII. [verse 257] An abstract of the Charles County Court Record concerning Henry Goodrick's assault upon John Lew, 14 September 1686, is presented in *"The Search for Survivors,"* op. cit., p. 4, citing [13.pdf #120]. See also "Dishonorable Mentions," in *"The Search for Survivors,"* p. 26.

XXVII. [verse 258] An abstract of the Charles County Court Record concerning Henry Thompson's abuse of Catherine Jones, 11 August 1691, is presented in *"The Search for Survivors,"* op. cit., p. 3, citing [17.pdf #139]. See also "Dishonorable Mentions," in *"The Search for Survivors,"* p. 28.

XXVII. [verse 258] Henry Thompson, servant to Thomas Clipsham, was brought to Charles County Court on 11 March 1679, adjudged to be sixteen years of age, and sentenced to seven years [09.pdf #82]. His expected date of freedom would have been 1686. Within four years he owned livestock, recording "his marke of cattle & hogges" 11 March 1690 [16.pdf #109], and within five years he was an overseer for Philip Lynes. (See "Encyclopedia of Survivors," in *"The Search for Survivors,"* op. cit., p. 146).

XXVII. [verse 259] Abstracts of the Charles County Court Records concerning James Lewis' alleged murder of Owen Carr, 14 January 1690 and 11 November 1690, are presented in *"The Search for Survivors,"* op. cit., p. 5. The records are at [16.pdf #112] and [17.pdf#83], the first citation being inadvertently omitted. See also "Dishonorable Mentions," in *"The Search for Survivors,"* p. 27.

XXVII. [verse 260] Abstracts of the Charles County Court Records concerning the ordeal of Adam Wharton, 9 December 1685 and 10 August 1686, are presented in *"The Search for Survivors,"* op. cit., p. 4, citing [13.pdf #47, #119]. As it happens, Adam Horton was an orphan, son of Joseph Horton, age not stated, bound to Philip Lines on 8 June 1675 [07.pdf #63]

XXVII. [verses 261-262] Abstracts of the Charles County Court Records concerning the ordeal of Teague Turlayes, 8 March 1697 and 8 June 1697, are presented in *"The Search for Survivors,"* op. cit., p. 4, citing [19.pdf #111, 131].

See also "Recaptured Runaways," p. 197, citing 10 November 1696 at [19.pdf #73], and "Abuse and Neglect," p. 248, citing 9 March 1697, 8 June 1697, and 9 November 1697, at [19.pdf #111, #131, #170], in *"The Search for Survivors."*

XXVII. [verses 263-266] Abstracts of the Charles County Court Records concerning Philip Lynes' continued abuse of Catherine Jones (also James Thornborough and Edward Darnell), 8 November 1691 and 10 November 1692, are presented in *"The Search for Survivors,"* op. cit., p. 3, citing [17.pdf #157, #276]. For a full page abstract see "Abuse and Neglect," p. 245, in *"The Search for Survivors."*

XXVIII. [verse 269] ref. *"Birth and Shipping Records,"* op. cit., p. xxix.

XXVIII. [verses 270-273] ref. *"The Search for Survivors,"* op. cit., pp. 1-3.

XXVIII. [verse 274] ref. *"The Search for Survivors,"* op. cit., p. 7, citing Last Will and Testament of Philip Lynes, probated 15 August 1709 at Liber AB No. 3 Folio 28.

XXVIII. [verse 275] Colonel John Seymour was the tenth Royal Governor of Maryland from 1704 to 1709. For a statement of the relationships of Madam Jean Seymour, Mrs. Mary Contee, and Captain Thomas Seymour to the Governor, ref. http://boards.ancestry.com/surnames.seymour/740/mb.ashx

XXVIII. [verses 275-276] Public Record Office, London, Colonial Office 5, Vol. 749. Shipping returns, Maryland. 1689-1702. Complete. Photostats. 282 prints in 5 parts, 447 equivalent pages. Received by Library of Congress February 7, 1939. Cited by Griffin, *"Guide to Manuscripts,"* op. cit.

William Bladen is identified in photostatic copies of actual shipping records as Royall Naval Officer, 1 November 1698, Port Annapolis; and Deputy Receiver, Port of Annapolis, 23 May 1698. ref. "Duties Paid for Imported White Servants," p. 343, and "Duties Paid for Imported Negro Slaves, pp. 354, 358, in *"Birth and Shipping Records,"* op. cit.

See also "Archives of Maryland, Historical List, Naval Officers, 1694-1777," http://msa.maryland.gov/msa/speccol/sc2600/sc2685/html/navoff.html

XXIX. [verse 277] Henry Hardy, "base child of Henry Howard and Issabell Hardy," Baptized 5 April 1646, Saint Peter, Burnley, Lancashire, England. ref. "Kids from Lancashire," in *"Birth and Shipping Records,"* op. cit., p. 69, citing *"OnLine Parish Clerks for the County of Lancashire"* http://www.lan-opc.org.uk/Search/indexp.html

XXIX. [verse 277] Henry Hardy, servant of Thomas Percei, was brought to Charles County Court on 2 July 1664 and adjudged to be twenty years of age, which equated to six years of servitude. [02.pdf #377]

XXIX. [verse 278] Henry Hardy was baptized in 1646. His expected date of freedom would have been in 1670. He was probably twenty-four years old. His master, Thomas Percey, died 5 November 1666. [03.pdf #297] ref. "Vital Records," in *"The Search for Survivors,"* op. cit., p. 270. We do not know with whom Henry Hardy completed his six years of servitude.

XXIX. [verse 278] On 10 November 1691, "Henry Hardy Gentleman" was sworn and admitted an attorney of the Charles County Court. [17.pdf #157] ref. *"The Search for Survivors,"* op. cit., p. 9.

XXIX. [verse 278] On 25 July 1696, "Capt. Henry Hardy" and nine others were "ordained and appointed" Worshippfull Commissioners for Charles County Court. [19.pdf #39] ref. *"The Search for Survivors,"* op. cit., p. 9.

XXIX. [verse 280] The probate case of Richard Ashman first appears in the Court Records on 4 October 1698. "Henry Hardy & Anne his wife" are named as the administrators of the estate of Richard Ashman. [19.pdf #256] ref. *"The Search for Survivors,"* op. cit., p. 10.

XXIX. [verse 280] The names and birth dates of the children of Richard and Ann Ashman are listed in the Charles County Court Records. [16.pdf #121] [22.pdf #129] ref. *"The Search for Survivors,"* op. cit., pp. 10, 251.

XXIX. [verse 280] On 10 March 1702, "Anne Hardy the wife of Capt. Henry Hardy" petitioned "that shee with her children may be permitted to live upon her owne land and to be allowd a sufficient maintenance to subsist upon" [22.pdf #4] ref. *"The Search for Survivors,"* op. cit., p. 10.

XXIX. [verse 281] Deed from Thomas Baker to Richard Ashman, for 50 acres at "ye head of a brooke called Bakers Creeke," dated 2 January 1678 [08.pdf #57]; Deed from John & Mary Dent to Richard Ashman for 140 acres contiguous to "Bakers Rest," dated 1 June 1678 [09.pdf #17]; and Deed from Richard and Anne Ashman to John Bayly for 100 acres contiguous to "Bakers Rest," dated 13 January 1680 [09.pdf #140]. ref. "Grantee Index to Deeds," in *"The Search for Survivors,"* op. cit., pp. 290, 291.

XXIX. [verse 281] "Capt. Henry Hardy" is named as one of the presiding judges at Charles County Court on 10 March 1702, the very day that his wife petitioned for legal separation. [22.pdf #2] ref. *"The Search for Survivors,"* op. cit., p. 10.

XXIX. [verse 282] On 10 August 1703, "Anne ye wife of Capt. Henry Hardy" filed a complaint against her said husbands harsh & ill usage of her children & desires that they may be taken away from him and that they may all be bound out to trades" [22.pdf #125] "Capt. Henry Hardy" was named as a presiding judge on that day. [22.pdf #124] ref. *"The Search for Survivors,"* op. cit., p. 10.

XXIX. [verse 283] "Capt. Henry Hardy" last appears as a presiding judge at Charles County Court on 12 June 1705. [23.pdf #76] He is not named on 14 August 1705 [23.pdf #88] or on any date thereafter.

XXIX. [verse 283] On 13 August 1706, "Anne Hardy the wife of Capt. Henry Hardy" filed a complaint "that through his harsh usage shee is not able to live and cohabbitt with him." Henry Hardy consented, in person, and agreed to provide her 1500 pounds of tobacco every year for life. [23.pdf #138]

XXIX. [verses 284-285] The deposition of Mary Symmons, brief but graphic, is transcribed in *"The Search for Survivors,"* op. cit., p. 11. [23.pdf #138]

XXIX. [verse 286] Henry Hardy was promptly acquitted. The Court was more interested in enslaving Margaret Macclannen. [23.pdf #138]

XXIX. [verse 287] On 10 September 1706. Henry Hardy had the temerity to bring Mary Symmons to court "to be adjudged for runaway time," but "the Court ordered that Mary Symmons be free from Capt. Henry Hardys service." ref. *"The Search for Survivors,"* op. cit., p. 12. [23.pdf #141]

XXX. [verse 290] The Last Will and Testament of Walter Bayne was dated 12 April 1670, and probated 28 May 1670 [Liber A No. 2 Folio 9]. In his will, he left to his "sonne John Beane" 1000 acres "in St. Maries County" and 450 acres in Charles County. ref. *"The Search for Survivors,"* op. cit., p. 13.

XXX. [verse 290] Walter Bayne first appears in the Charles County Court Records as deceased on 12 September 1671. His widow Ellinor Bayne is named as Administratrix [06.pdf #49]. ref. "Index to Deaths and Estates," pp. 334-335, in *"The Search for Survivors,"* op. cit.

XXX. [verse 291] John Waterworth, son of William Waterworth, Baptized 2 February 1668, Saint Mary the Virgin, Blackburn, Lancashire (ref. *"Birth and Shipping Records,"* op. cit., p. 76), was brought to Charles County Court by John Bayne on 8 August 1682 and adjudged to be twelve years of age [10.pdf #177], which equated to ten years of servitude.

XXX. [verse 292] Daniell Linghams, servant to John Bayne, and Samuell Burgesse, servant to Mrs. Elinor Bayne, presented by John Bayne her son, 11 March 1690. Both had Indentures judged not "good and authentick," and their ages were not adjudged. [16.pdf #114] ref. *"The Search for Survivors,"* op. cit., p. 75.

XXX. [verses 293-294] ref. *"The Search for Survivors,"* op. cit., p. 14, citing Charles County Court Record, 10 June 1690 [17.pdf #18].

XXX. [verse 295] ref. *"The Search for Survivors,"* op. cit., p. 15, citing Charles County Court Records, 14 December 1690 and 11 August 1691 [17.pdf #99, #138].

XXX. [verse 296] ref. *"The Search for Survivors,"* op. cit., p. 15, citing Charles County Court Records, 8 November 1692 [17.pdf #275, #276].

XXX. [verse 297] ref. *"The Search for Survivors,"* op. cit., p. 16, footnote [29].

XXX. [verse 298] ref. *"The Search for Survivors,"* op. cit., p. 16, citing Charles County Court Records, 31 January 1693 [18.pdf #24].

XXX. [verse 299] Patrick Morand and Patrick Cusack, "two Irish servants," were brought to St. Mary's County Court by John Bayne on 1 August 1693 and adjudged to be thirteen and seventeen years of age. respectively. Mr. John Bayne himself sitting on the bench as one of the "Gentleman Justices," passing judgment upon his own "servants." The order is transcribed in the Charles County Court Records, 11 March 1701 [21.pdf #92]. ref. *"The Search for Survivors,"* op. cit., p. 16.

XXX. [verse 300] ref. *"The Search for Survivors,"* op. cit., p. 17, citing Charles County Court Records, 9 June 1696 [19.pdf #38].

XXX. [verse 301] ref. *"The Search for Survivors,"* op. cit., p. 17, citing Charles County Court Records, 9 November 1697 [19.pdf #169].

XXX. [verse 302] Alexander Mills, 1 February 1698 [19.pdf #186]; John Bryan, Anthony Coney, John Morrough (Magrah), 19 April 1698 [19.pdf #206]; John Rye, 8 August 1699 [20.pdf #79].

XXX. [verse 303] John Bayne is first identified as "Capt. John Bayne" on 11 August 1696 [19.pdf #40], right after he became Sheriff.

XXX. [verse 304] Charles Daniellson, age 14, Alexander Faulkner, age 14, Alexander Ross, age 18, 4 April 1699 [20.pdf #27].

XXX. [verse 304] John Cameright, age 8, 14 November 1699 [20.pdf #99].

XXX. [verse 305] Gerrard Fowke, successor to John Bayne. was sworn as Sheriff on 8 August 1699 [20.pdf # 79].

XXX. [verse 305] Capt. John Bayne was named as a presiding judge at Charles County Court on 12 March 1700, 13 August 1700, and 10 September 1700 [21.pdf #2, #17, #40].

XXX. [verses 306-307] Last Will and Testament of Captain John Bayne, dated 5 October 1700, proved 25 October 1701 (Land Office, Annapolis, Maryland, Wills, Liber TB No. 11, folio 217). On 5 December 1701, Thomas Whichaley, formerly Deputy Sheriff to Capt. John Bayne, was asked how the will "comes to be soe much blotted and interlined." He swore that all the changes to the will were made and approved by John Bayne himself, and that he "offered to write it over" "saying it should all be of one hand writing," "but Mr. Bayne answered him passionately that if he staid soe long he should not be able to goe at all he being just then goeing down to St. Georges to take shipping for England and his horses then up and himselfe then ready to goe." (Land Office, Annapolis, Maryland, Wills, Liber TB No. 11, Folio 248).

XXX. [verse 308] Last Will and Testament of Ellinor Bayne, dated 21 November 1700 (Land Office, Annapolis, Maryland, Wills, Liber A No. 2 Folio 232).

XXXI. [verses 309-312] ref. map of St. Mary's County and vicinity, published by Simon J. Martenet, 1866, showing the route from Port Tobacco to Saint George's Island, the route of Captain John Bayne's last journey. https://www.oldmapsonline.org/map/rumsey/2517.019

XXXI. [verses 313-314] "Mr. John Bayne of Verginia" was buried 27 February 1701, ref. *"The Earliest Registers of the Parish of Liverpool, St. Nicholas Church, 1660 to 1704,"* University of Liverpool, 1909, p. 200. NOTE: These are the Bishop's Transcripts. I was unaware of them when *"The Search for Survivors"* was published, and incorrectly stated on p. 21 that his death was unconfirmed. https://archive.org/details/earliestregister00live/page/n12

XXXII. [verse 315] "I doe hereby ordaine Constitute and appoint my Trusty and well beloved wife Anne Bayne my whole and sole Executrix of this my last will and Testament" (Last Will and Testament of Captain John Bayne, op. cit.)

XXXII. [verses 316-318] Col. John Courts appeared at Charles County Court on behalf of the orphan John Warren on 11 November 1701 [21.pdf #160].

XXXII. [verse 319] John Bayne last appeared at Charles County Court "in his proper person" on 10 September 1700 [21.pdf #40]. Not until 10 March 1702 do these words appear in the Court Records: "Anne Bayne Executrix of the Last Will and Testament of John Bayne Deceased" [22.pdf #9, #10]. Three weeks later, this explanation is given: "and the said John Bayne is since dead as by the insinuation of Anne Bayne." My Funk & Wagnalls dictionary defines the verb to "insinuate" as "to indicate indirectly, as if by devious, artful, and questionable means." ref. *"The Search for Survivors,"* op. cit., p. 21.

XXXII. [verse 320] John Bayne bequeathed 1550 acres to his son Ebsworth; 200 or 300 acres to his daughter Anne; and 1700 or 1800 acres to his son Walter. (ref. Last Will and Testament of Captain John Bayne, op. cit.)

XXXII. [verse 320] ref. Inventory of Capt. John Bayne, 10 July 1702, in "Inventories and Accounts, Liber 22, 1702-1703, Folios 32-36, Hall of Records, Maryland State Archives. Sixteen white servants are mentioned, thirteen by name, including: John Bryon, Anthony Cony, and John Mograugh, each identified as "a servant boy neare 5 yrs to serve," and James Rye, "a servant boy neare 6 yrs to serve," listed between the Negroes and the cows (Folio 34); and Alexander Mills, "a servant boy 3 yrs & 8 mo to serve," listed between the bulls and the horses (Folio 36).

XXXII. [verse 321] Not named or mentioned in the Inventory of Capt. John Bayne, op. cit., are five Scots-Irish servants without indentures, all of whom had previously appeared in the Charles County Court Records: Charles Daniellson, age 15, Alexander Faulkner, age 14, and Alexander Ross, age 18, all on 4 April 1699 [20.pdf #27]; Patrick Cusack, age 17, and Patrick Morand, age 13, both on 11 March 1701 [21.pdf #92]. Col. John Courts stated on **11 November 1701** that "Capt. John Bayne hath leased the said Warren's plantation to William Hawton Junior who hath five servants and himselfe who clears and destroyes the land." [21.pdf # 160]

XXXII. [verses 321-322] ref. Inventory of Madam Anne Bayne, 15 July 1703, in "Inventories and Accounts, Liber 24, 1703-1704, Folios 134-140, Hall of Records, Maryland State Archives. Among the white servants named are James Rye "having to serve 4 yrs next month," listed between the Negroes and the horses (Folio 138); Alex Mills "2 yeares next May" (Folio 139); and Anthony Cony, John Bryan, and John Magrah, all "to serve 3 yrs next month," listed between the sows and the Negroes (Folio 140).

XXXII. [verse 323] John Bryan did not get free until 9 March 1708, when Patrick Moreland was summoned "to give evidence between John Bryan and Mr. Walter Bayne" [23.pdf #236]. John Bryan had served ten years, or nearly so, and was now the servant of Walter Bayne, administrator of the estate of Anne Bayne deceased [23.pdf #90]. The Court heard Patrick Moreland, and ordered that "John Bryan be free from the service of Walter Bayne," "John Bryan quitting his freedom dues which he is willing to do" [23.pdf #236]. ref. *"The Search for Survivors,"* op. cit., p. 24.

XXXII. [verse 324] *"The Search for Survivors,"* op. cit., p. 24. Family legend at http://boards.ancestry.com/thread.aspx?mv=flat&m=247&p=surnames.obryan

PART THREE

XXXIII. [verses 325-329] William D. Keel, "Transcription of Germantown Friends' Protest Against Slavery, 1688," in *"Yearbook of German-American Studies 23"* (1988): 219-22 (with Helmut Huelsbergen). University of Kansas Scholar Works, https://kuscholarworks.ku.edu/handle/1808/13386

XXXIV. [verse 330] Pennsylvania Charter to William Penn, 4 March 1681

XXXIV. [verse 330] "In 1682, (William) Penn, with 2,000 settlers, mostly like himself, Friends (Quakers), arrived, and laid out Philadelphia." ref. *"Quarterly Register of the American Education Society,"* Vol. III, Perkins & Marvin, Boston, 1831, Religious Denominations – Pennsylvania, p. 211.

XXXIV. [verse 331] "1682. 9 10th mo. The Antelope of Bellfast arrived here from Ireland." ref. J. Smith Futhey and Gilbert Cope, "Arrivals Between 1682 and 1688," in *"History of Chester County, Pennsylvania,"* Louis H. Everts, Philadelphia, 1881, p. 22. https://archive.org/details/cu31924005813518
See also "A Partial List of the Families Who Arrived at Philadelphia between 1682 and 1687," in *"The Pennsylvania Magazine of History and Biography,"* Vol. 8, No. 3, October 1884, Historical Society of Pennsylvania, University of Pennsylvania, p. 329. https://archive.org/details/jstor-20084664/page/n1

Edward Cooke is identified as the Master in Dobson, David, *"Ships from Ireland to Early America, 1623-1850,"* Genealogical Publishing Company, 1999.

XXXIV. [verse 332] "Proo Matharoon, servt. to Natha. Bacon Esq. imported in the Antelope of Bellfast in James river, adjudged sixteen years of age and is ordered to serve according to Act." (York County, Virginia, Deeds, Orders, Wills, No. 6, 24 June 1679. On microfilm at the Virginia State Library. ref. *"Without Indentures,"* op. cit., p. 215).

XXXIV. [verse 333] Arrived 6 August 1683. Ship and commander (*Concord of London*, William Jefferies) named in Letter from James Claypoole to William Penn, 1 April 1683, London, reprinted in Soderland, Jean R., *"William Penn and the Founding of Pennsylvania, 1680-1684, A Documentary History,"* University of Pennsylvania Press, Philadelphia, 1983, p. 210. See also *"Supplement to the Trilogy,"* op. cit., p. 68.

XXXIV. [verse 333] Stephen Saunders Webb, *"1676: The End of American Independence,"* Syracuse University Press, 1984, 1995, p. 104. https://books.google.com/books?isbn=0815603614

XXXIV. [verse 334] The *Concord of London*, Capt. Thomas Grantham Commander, was named in York County Court by twenty-one kids without indentures, always in winter: three in 1675, nine in 1675/1676, four in 1678, three in 1679, and two in 1680 (ref. *"Without Indentures,"* op. cit., pp. 205-223). The youngest was William Garrow, eight years old, from Plymouth, Devon, England (ref. *"Birth and Shipping Records,"* op. cit., p. 120). And there may have been more. There were four other jurisdictions on the James River at this time (1675-1680) – Elizabeth City, James City, New Kent County, and Gloucester County (ref. Interactive Map of Virginia County Formation History, https://www.mapofus.org/virginia). The court records are lost for all of these.

XXXIV. [verse 335] The *Golden Fortune* and/or Capt. William Jeffreys Commander, was named in Middlesex or York County Court by six kids without indentures: two in April or May 1678, and four in February or March 1679 (ref. *"Without Indentures,"* op. cit., pp. 192, 206, 209, 211, 221). The *Sarah*, William Jeffreys Commander, was named in Middlesex or York County Court by three kids without indentures: one in August 1693, one in October 1696, and one in February 1701 (ref. *"Without Indentures,"* op. cit., pp. 193, 213, 214). William Jefferys or Jefferies commanded the *Golden Fortune* in December 1677 (Survey Report No. 6002, p. 36) and in January 1678 (Survey Report No. 6045, p. 1). ref. *"Virginia Colonial Records, 1607-1853,"* Middlesex County Record Office, presented courtesy of the Library of Virginia. https://search.ancestry.com/search/db.aspx?dbid=61473

XXXIV. [verse 336] "The Jeffries Thomas Arnold m(aste)r from London Arrived 20 1st mo. 1686." ref. "Arrivals Between 1682 and 1688," op. cit., p. 22, and "A Partial List of the Families," op. cit., p. 329.

XXXIV. [verse 336] "John Le Marr, Servt, to Christr: Robinson, coming into this Countrey in ye Shipp, "Jeffryes," without Indenture is adjudged fifteen years of age & is ordered to serve according to Law." (Middlesex County Order Book, 2 February 1685. ref. *"Without Indentures,"* op. cit., p. 196).

XXXIV. [verse 336] Thomas Arnold (a.k.a. Arnell) commanded the *Jefferies (Jeffreys, Jeffereyes)* in August 1684 (Survey Report No. 2152, p. 2), September 1684 (Survey Report No. 2152, p. 8), in October and November 1688 (Survey Report No. 4792, p. 2 and No. 7466, p. 2), in June 1689 (Survey Report No. 6832, p. 1), in July 1691 (Survey Report No. 7343, p.2), in October 1691 (Survey Report No. 6837, p. 3 and No. 7343, p. 4). ref. *"Virginia Colonial Records, 1607-1853,"* op. cit. See also *"Supplement to the Trilogy,"* op. cit., p. 68.

XXXIV. [verse 337] The *Richard and Jane* -- or *John* (sic), Thomas Arnall Commander, was named in York County Court by two kids without indentures: one on 25 January 1675, one on 24 March 1675 (ref. *"Without Indentures,"* op. cit., pp. 208, 222). The *Henry and Anne* (or *Ann*) and/or Thomas Arnold (or Arnall) Commander, was named in Middlesex or York County Court by fifteen kids without indentures: one in February 1676, six in February or March 1678, and eight in January 1679 or March 1679 (ref. *"Without Indentures,"* op. cit., pp. 191-200, 205-223). Thomas Arnold (a.k.a. Arnall) commanded the *Richard and Jane* in September 1672 (Survey Report No. 4407, p. 2, and No. 4408, p. 5), February 1674 (Survey Report No. 7460, p. 2), and November 1674 (Survey Report No. 6591, p. 2). Thomas Arnold commanded the *Henry and Anne* in September 1675 (Survey Report No. 3963, p. 7), in November 1676 (Survey Report No. 5868, p. 27), in October 1677 (No. 5860, p. 4, No. 5864, p. 8, and Survey Report No. 6002, pp. 5, 27, 28,), December 1677 (Survey Report No. 6750, p. 5), and September 1678 (Survey Report No. 6004, p. 5, and No. 6045, p. 5). ref. *"Virginia Colonial Records, 1607-1853"* op. cit.

XXXIV. [verse 338] ref. *"Birth and Shipping Records,"* op. cit., p. 306.

XXXV. [verse 339] "28th 11th mo. 1687. The Margaret from London arrived here from London John Bowman commander." "the Eliza: & Mary, John Bowman M(aste)r arrived here ye 22d 7th mo. 1683." (ref. "Arrivals Between 1682 and 1688," op. cit., p. 22; and "A Partial List of the Families," op. cit., p. 330). See also *"Supplement to the Trilogy,"* op. cit., p. 68.

XXXV. [verse 340] "John Tucker, servant to Mr. John Page, imported in the Pelicaine, is adjudged age 17." 10 November 1670. "Mary Barrosone (?), servant to Capt. John Underhill, imported in the Pelicaine is adjudged age 17." 10 January 1671. (York County, Virginia, Deeds, Orders, Wills).

XXXV. [verse 341] *"Virginia Colonial Records, 1607-1853,"* op. cit. When my previous books were written, this database did not turn up on ancestry.com unless the user entered the exact words of the title. As of this writing, one can drill down to it by entering "United States," "Virginia," and "1600s." The records are incorporated at *"Supplement to the Trilogy,"* op. cit., pp. 52-66.

XXXV. [verse 341] John Bowman commanded the *Pelican* in March 1672 (Survey Report No. 3964, p. 22), in November 1672 (Survey Report No. 4408, p. 21), and in March 1673 (Survey Report No. 5113, p. 1). ref. *"Virginia Colonial Records, 1607-1853,"* op. cit. He also transported a servant named Abigail Yates, coming from London "in ye good ship called ye Pelican of London Captn. John Bowman Comander," arriving on 2 June 1674 with indentures for four years (ref. *"The Search for Survivors,"* op. cit., pp. 56, 113, citing Charles County Court Records, 14 August 1678 [09.pdf #38].

XXXV. [verse 342] John Bowman commanded the *Elizabeth & Mary* in 1681 (Survey Report No. 10069, p. 1) and in May 1684 (Survey Report not numbered). ref. *"Virginia Colonial Records, 1607-1853,"* op. cit.

XXXV. [verse 342] Joseph Oldfield, servant to Coll. George Reade Esqr., "who arrived about a weeke in Capt. Thomas Varbell's shipp called the Elizabeth & Mary," was adjudged "to be about 15 years of age and soe to serve till hee is 21." York County, Virginia, Deeds, Orders, Wills, 25 February 1658. Henry Manwaring, servant to Thomas Jarrell, "who came into this Countrey this present yeare in the shipp, Elizabeth and Mary, Thomas Stringer, Master" was adjudged to be twelve years of age and so to serve until the age of 24. Surry County, Virginia, Court Records, 9 November 1703.

XXXV. [verse 343] The photostatic copies of shipping records at the Library of Congress (Public Record Office, London, Colonial Office 5, Vol. 749. Shipping returns, Maryland, 1689-1702, op. cit.) list five voyages to Maryland by the *Margarett of London* between 1692 and 1698. On 1 November 1698, import duties were paid on 43 "servants" by Abraham Trickett (ref. *"Birth and Shipping Records,"* op. cit., pp. 11, 310, 343).

XXXV. [verse 344] John Bowman transported "into this Countrey" at least seven servants, and by his Oath "hee had ye counterparts of their Indentures & did reade them aboard of his ship at Gravesend, and they were kidnappers Indentures" ref. *"The Search for Survivors,"* op. cit., pp. 25, 33, citing Charles County Court Records, 10 June 1690 [17.pdf #18].

XXXV. [verse 346] "that would be as near (to) heaven as he ever expected to get." ref. W. W. H. Davis, "The History of Bucks County, Pennsylvania, Chapter XXIX, Upper Makefield," 1876 and 1905 editions.
http://files.usgwarchives.net/pa/bucks/history/local/davis/davis29.txt

XXXVI. [verse 347] "noe proofe appearing here in Court that ye said Indentures were signed sealed & delivered by ye said John Williams with whom they did indent, & ye same not being under ye seale of an Office, or under ye hand of any Justice of ye peace" ref. *"The Search for Survivors,"* op. cit., p. 33, citing Charles County Court Records, 10 June 1690 [17.pdf #18].

XXXVI. [verse 348] "And it appeareing by ye Oath of Mr. John Bowman who transported them into this Countrey that hee had ye counterparts of their Indentures & did reade them aboard of his ship at Gravesend, and they were kidnappers Indentures" ref. *"The Search for Survivors,"* op. cit., p. 33, citing Charles County Court Records, 10 June 1690 [17.pdf #18].

XXXVI. [verse 349] ref. *"The Search for Survivors,"* op. cit., p. 33, citing Charles County Court Records, 12 January 1686, 9 February 1686, 9 March 1686 [13.pdf #47, #48, #49]. Two produced indentures which the Court found invalid. Two others did not appear in Court until 10 June 1690 [17.pdf #18]

XXXVI. [verse 350] John Williams commanded the *Judith* in December 1683 (Survey Report No. 2151, p. 5), and the *Elizabeth* in August 1685 (Survey Report No. 10238, p. 1), in May 1686 (Survey Report No. 10242, p. 4), in August 1686 (Survey Report No. 10242, p. 5), and in April 1690 (Survey Report No. 10273, p. 2). ref. *"Virginia Colonial Records, 1607-1853,"* op. cit.

XXXVI. [verse 351] "Habell Dibdon, 16, of Middlesex, to John Williams. 9 years. *Judith.* 6 December 1683." (Survey Report No. 2151, p. 5). ref. *"Virginia Colonial Records, 1607-1853,"* op. cit.

XXXVI. [verse 352] Survey Report No. 2151, pp. 1-8, in *"Virginia Colonial Records, 1607-1853,"* op. cit. Habell Dibdon was 16 years of age. If he had arrived without indentures he would have served five years in Virginia or seven years in Maryland (ref. *"Without Indentures,"* op. cit., pp. x-xi).

XXXVI. [verse 353] "Mary Gray, imported in the Judith, Capt. Mathew Trim, Comander, servt to Mr. John Gawin, is adjudged seventeen years of age and ordered to serve according to act." (York County, Virginia, Deeds, Orders, Wills, 26 May 1684. On microfilm at the Virginia State Library. ref. *"Without Indentures,"* op. cit., p. 211).

XXXVI. [verses 354-356] "Sessions 24 Aug. 1 James II (1682) True Bill: Mathew Trim and Sarah Falconer assaulted Elizabeth Partridge, conveyed her aboard *The Indee,* transported her to Virginia, and sold her." (Survey Report No. 2178, p. 3) ref. *"Virginia Colonial Records, 1607-1853,"* op. cit.

XXXVI. [verse 356] "Richard Kitchinger imported in the good shippe ye Indy, Capt. Trim Comander servant to John Tomer is adjudged to be fiveteen years of age & is ordered to serve according to Act" (York County, Virginia, Deeds, Orders, Wills, 24 June 1686. On microfilm at the Virginia State Library. ref. *"Without Indentures,"* op. cit., p. 214).

XXXVI. [verse 357] "Minutes, Friday 28 June 1689: Protection granted to the Companies of these ships, at the request of their owners, lately returned from Virginia, to pass from the Isle of Wight to the Thames: Wm. Jeffrey, *Concord*, 40 men; Zach. Taylor, *Augustin*, 35 men; Math. Trim, *Judith*, 20 men; Edward Audley, *Jacob*, 15 men; Thos. Arnold, *Jeffreys*, 36 men; Jn. Adkins, *Samuel*, 13 men; Rich. Tribbott, *Ann and Mary*, 16 men." (Survey Report No. 6832, p. 1) ref. *"Virginia Colonial Records, 1607-1853,"* op. cit.

XXXVI. [verse 358] Survey Report No. 2157, 2158, 2160, 2161, 2162, 2163, 2164, 2169, 2170, 2171, 2172, 2173, 2174, 2175, 2176, 2177, and 2178, the last containing three pages with twenty-one entries for kidnapping. All are transcribed in *"Supplement to the Trilogy,"* op. cit., pp. 48-51.

XXXVI. [verse 358] "Elizabeth Hamlyn was committed to the House of Correction for taking children in the streets and selling them to be carried off to Virginia." (Survey Report No. 2158) "George Lee committed on a charged of sending the son of Richard Medley to Barbados." (Survey Report No. 2161) "Margaret Geery ordered committed to prison on a charge of combining to convey Richard Hornold (aged 4) into Virginia." (Survey Report No. 2162) ref. *"Virginia Colonial Records, 1607-1853,"* op. cit.

XXXVI. [verse 359] "Sessions 28 Aug. 12 Chas. II (1660). Recognizances for appearance of Margery Staples to answer for selling her servant Ann Parker to be a slave in Virginia. 7 Aug. 12 Chas. II." (Survey Report No. 2175). ref. *"Virginia Colonial Records, 1607-1853,"* op. cit.

XXXVII. [verse 362] For a county by county listing of what records have survived, see "Pennsylvania Court Records," compiled by Stephanie Hoover. http://www.pennsylvaniaresearch.com/PennsylvaniaRecordSearches.html

XXXVII. [verse 363] Edwin B. Bronner, *"Philadelphia County Court of Quarter Sessions and Common Pleas, 1695."* The last full session on record is the "Court of Quarter Sessions held at Philadelphia the Third day of Septr 1695." https://journals.psu.edu/pmhb/article/download/31134/30889

XXXVII. [verses 362-363] *"Record of the Courts of Chester County Pennsylvania, 1681-1697,"* Published by the Colonial Society of Pennsylvania, Printed by Patterson & White Company, Philadelphia, 1910. https://search.ancestry.com/search/db.aspx?dbid=10698

XXXVII. [verse 364] Appearing at Chester County Court on 3 October 1693 were James Canide, James Driver, James Hercules, George Leacy, Daniell MackDeniell, Alexander Mecany, Alexander Ross, and Magnis Simson. All were children aged 11 to 14 "that Mauris Trent brought in to this Country." (ref. *"Record of the Courts of Chester County,"* op. cit., Vol. 1, p. 300.) All court records of children without indentures in the Delaware River Valley (Chester County, PA, Bucks County, PA, Burlington County, NJ and Kent County, DE) are abstracted in *"Supplement to the Trilogy,"* op. cit., pp. 69-77.

XXXVII. [verse 365] Appearing at Chester County Court on 1 October 1695 were Robert Flatt, Andrew Fraisor, James Johnson, John Mackellfray, and Henery Nickols. All were "brought in by Maurice Trent." (ref. *"Record of the Courts of Chester County,"* op. cit., Vol. 1, p. 355.)

XXXVII. [verse 366] "East New Jersey and the Delaware Valley," in *"Scottish Emigration to Colonial America, 1607-1785,"* by David Dobson, University of Georgia Press, 1994, pp. 53-54.

XXXVII. [verse 367] Appearing at Chester County Court were thirty-one children without indentures on 14 September 1697, eleven on 5 October 1697, and thirteen on 14 December 1697. (ref. *"Record of the Courts of Chester County,"* op. cit., Vol. 2, pp. 6-13). The entries for seventeen who appeared in October and December bear the notation that their sentences of servitude were to run "from the 14th day of September last past," thus suggesting that at least forty-eight were transported at the same time.

XXXVII. [verse 368] Children without indentures appeared at this time in adjacent counties of the Delaware River Valley: two at Bucks County, Pennsylvania on 5 October 1697; two at Kent County, Delaware on 10 August 1697 and 9 November 1697; and five at Burlington County, New Jersey on 21 July 1697, 9 August 1697, and 3 November 1697. All those at Burlington County were purchased "from James Trent."

"Records of the Courts of Quarter Sessions and Common Pleas of Bucks County, Pennsylvania 1684-1700"
https://search.ancestry.com/search/db.aspx?dbid=14303

"The Burlington court book: a record of Quaker jurisprudence in West New Jersey, 1680-1709" https://search.ancestry.com/search/db.aspx?dbid=13867

"Court Records of Kent County, Delaware, 1680-1705," edited by Leon DeValinger, Jr., State Archivist of Delaware, American Historical Association, Washington, D.C., 1959.

It is apparent from the court records that these children were to serve until the age of twenty-one. Altogether, 103 were brought to court in these four counties between 1693 and 1700. Of these, 66 had their ages adjudged, or else their terms of servitude were stated, from which we can deduce their ages. There were forty-four boys under fourteen years of age, and one girl under twelve years of age, all of whom, by law, were too young to sign an indenture. If they were to be "servants," they had to be kidnapped. (ref. "Age of Consent," in *"Birth and Shipping Records,"* op. cit., p. xxix).

XXXVII. [verse 369] Last Will and Testament of James Trent, Merchant, dated 30 October 1697, proved 29 July 1698, in *"Philadelphia County, Pennsylvania, Will Index, 1682-1819,"* Historical Society of Pennsylvania, 1900. https://www.ancestry.com/search/collections/philpa1682

XXXVII. [verse 370] After the end of the child trafficking careers of Maurice Trent and James Trent, the trade became centered once again at the Chesapeake Bay. In the surviving court records of colonial Maryland and Virginia, the children without indentures are 67 in 1697, 235 in 1698, and 677 in 1699 (ref. *"Without Indentures,"* op. cit., p. xiii).

XXXVIII. [verse 371] The residence of James Trent is identified in his Last Will and Testament as Inverness, Murrayshire, Scotland. (ref. *"Philadelphia County, Pennsylvania, Will Index, 1682-1819,"* op. cit.) "The Trents seem to have been engaged in shipping children, some unwillingly, to America. James and Maurice Trent, sons of William Trent in Inverness and nephews of Maurice Trent in Leith, settled in **Philadelphia, Pennsylvania, before 1681**" (ref. David Dobson, *"Scottish Emigration to Colonial America,"* op. cit., p. 52).

XXXVIII. [verse 372] A diligent search of the parish registers has revealed the birth places of twenty-one of the children transported to the Delaware River Valley (ref. *"Supplement to the Trilogy,"* op. cit., pp. 78-80). Among them are:

Flett, Robert, Baptized 24 January 1681, Kirkwall, Orkney, Scotland
Symondsone, Magnus, Baptized 14 October 1680, Kirkwall, Orkney, Scotland
Tait, Magnus, Baptized 1681 or 1682, Kirkwall, Orkney, Scotland
Hercules, James, Born c. 1680, Shetland Islands
Camrone, Daniell, Born c. 1685, Hebrides Islands
Mattson, Aneus, Born c. 1683, Hebrides Islands

XXXVIII. [verse 373] Lydias Dobie, Alexander Frizall, and William Johnstowne, of Edinburgh; John Seller, of Stirling; William Clunie of Perth; Patrick Gourdoun, of Aberdeen; Andrew Fraser, of Inverness; Margaret Finley, of Northumberland; John Maston, Hugh Willson, Benjamin More, and Reese Price, of London; George Lacy and Henry Nicholls, of Devon; Thomas Bullen, of Cheshire; John Anderson, of Dublin.

XXXVIII. [verse 374] Maurice Trent is said to have died 7 October 1697 in Pennsylvania. I cannot find proof of this. But the Last Will and Testament of his brother James Trent, dated 23 days later, 30 October 1697, does leave his whole estate to William Trent.

XXXVIII. [verses 375-376] "Meet William Trent," The 1719 William Trent House Museum, https://williamtrenthouse.org/about/meet-william-trent/

XXXVIII. [verse 376] The list of more than forty sailing ships owned by William Trent appeared in the *Philadelphia Business Directory of 1703*, and was reprinted in the *American Historical Register*, April 1895, pp. 730-731.
https://books.google.com/books?id=1YA3AQAAMAAJ
https://books.google.com/books?id=fQQ7AQAAIAAJ

XXXVIII. [verse 377] Proof that William Trent's ships were used for child trafficking: *Sarah*, identified in court records of York County, 1689, 1693, 1701. *Mary*, identified in court records of Somerset County, 1691, 1708. *Globe of London*, Duty paid by Capt. Bartholomew Watts, 15 Servants, May 1698. *Diligence of London*, Duty paid by Capt. Isaac Wyle, 7 Servants, 26 March 1698. *Dove*, identified in court records of Northumberland County, 1706. *Jane*, identified in court records of Northumberland County, 1700. *Happy Union*, Duty paid by Capt. John Browne, 59 Servants, 26 March 1698. *Susannah*, identified in court records of Middlesex County, 1690. *Richard & Sarah*, Duty paid by Capt. Edw. Andley, 29 Servants, 27 April 1698. (ref. *"Without Indentures,"* op. cit., pp. 253-256; and *"Birth and Shipping Records,"* op. cit., pp. 303, 305, 306, 315-316).

XXXVIII. [verse 379] For an annual breakdown of the numbers for Maryland and Virginia, see *"Without Indentures,"* op. cit., p. xiii. Thirty-eight additional names are presented in *"Birth and Shipping Records,"* op. cit., pp. 369-371.

XXXIX. [verse 382] In Chester County, Pennsylvania, only ten men owned more than one child. Eight were Quakers: Thomas Cartwright (2), Francis Chadsey (2), Joseph Coeburn (2), Jeremiah Collett (2), William Collett (3), William Davis (2), Evan Prother (2), Caleb Pusey (3). The others were Justice Jasper Yeates (3), and Maurice Trent, the child trafficker (2). Fifty-four men and two women (Margaret Green and Elizabeth Withers) bought one child each. Many of these may have been, in effect, adoptions.

XXXIX. [verse 383] Fifteen of the children were to serve until the age of twenty-one "if taught to read and write." Otherwise, six months or one year would be deducted from their terms of service. This provision never once appears in the court records of colonial Maryland or Virginia.

XXXIX. [verse 383] Alexander Stewart, former servant to Francis Chadsey, was assigned to Henry Nayl. The court record explicitly states: "the said boy consents and agrees to serve the said Nayl one year and a quarter above his time by record if the said Henry Nayl teach hime the trade of a shoemaker" (ref. *"Record of the Courts of Chester County,"* op. cit., 10 June 1701).

XXXIX. [verse 384] Alexander Mickener, servant to Thomas Smith, "who having run away from his Master and for other misdemeniors as alsoe atempting to kill himselfe and for what charges he put his master to," ordered to serve "eight months after the expiration of his time if he behave himselfe well or else to sarve 10 months after" (ref. *"Record of the Courts of Chester County,"* op. cit., 5 August 1697).

XXXIX. [verse 385] Peter Hood, servant to Henry Lewis, was "indicted for stealing a bay gelding of the price of six pounds from the goods & chattels of John Wade," pleaded guilty, was ordered to "be whipt with ten lashes on his bare back and wear a Roman T according to law" and to "Pay to his said Master eighteen pounds at the expiration of his time of servitude and serve seventy eight days for runaway time" (ref. *"Record of the Courts of Chester County,"* op. cit., 25 November 1707 and 24 February 1708).

There are twenty-two recaptured runaway servants in the court records of Chester County. Only two, Alexander Mickener (Mecany) and Peter Hood, were without indentures.

XXXIX. [verse 386] Alexander Frasell (Freezell), ordered to serve until March 1704 or September 1704, was married in Marblehead, Essex, Massachusetts on 10 January 1704. Benjamin More, ordered to serve until December 1695, was married in Burlington County, New Jersey on 4 November 1693. Barbara Thompson, ordered to serve until December 1702, was married in Philadelphia, Pennsylvania on 19 July 1702. All thirteen marriage records, matched up with the court records ordering them into servitude, are abstracted in *"Supplement to the Trilogy,"* op. cit., pp. 81-82).

XXXIX. [verse 386] There are no petitions for freedom or complaints of abuse or neglect in the court records of Chester County from any of the seventy-nine children without indentures.

XXXIX. [verse 387] Former children without indentures who received land warrants in Chester County included: Thomas Bollen (200 acres, Nantmeal, 16 December 1736); James Bruce (185 acres, East Caln, 5 February 1734); John Davidson (250 acres, West Caln, 29 January 1733); John Davidson (215 acres, West Caln, 30 May 1748); Robert Gibbs (from John Martin, 100 acres,

West Caln, 5 April 1745); John Martin (to Robert Gibbs, 100 acres, West Caln, 5 April 1745); John Robinson (200 acres, West Caln, 23 February 1733); Magnus Simonson (150 acres, Birmingham, 3 September 1735); Magnus Simonson (100 acres, West Caln, 17 April 1738); Robert Sinclair (250 acres, Nantmeal, 10 May 1737); John Williamson (10 acres, New Town, 16 December 1736); and John Williamson (120 acres, Nottingham, 10 April 1746); John Young (150 acres, Bradford, 20 July 1744). See *"Records of the Land Office, Warrant Registers, 1733-1957,"* Pennsylvania Historical and Museum Commission, Pennsylvania State Archives

http://www.phmc.state.pa.us/bah/dam/rg/di/r17-88 WarrantRegisters/ChesterPages/r17-88ChesterPageInterface.htm

Former children without indentures appearing on Chester County Tax Lists between 1715 and 1741 are: John Anderson, James Bruce, John Davison, George Douglass, Alexander Hunter, Alexander Moore, Benjamin Moore, Reece Preece/Price, Thomas Robinson, Alexander Ross, Robert Scott, Magnus Simpson/Simonson, Robert Sinkler, George Slater, Magnus Tate, Thomas Taylor, John Williamson, Hugh Willson. (ref. **"Chester County Tax and Landowner Lists,"** http://www.chester.pa-roots.com/taxlists/index.html)

Eight former children without indentures appear on these tax lists but had no deeds to their land. None of them are listed after the year 1730, which suggests that they were among the migrants to the Cumberland Valley.

XXXIX. [verses 389-394] Personal communication, Luke Martin, Parishville, New York. Supporting documentation is found in John Landis Ruth, *"The Earth is the Lord's: A Narrative History of the Lancaster Mennonite Conference,"* Herald Press, Harrisonburg, Pennsylvania, 2001, pp. 224, 276.

XL. [verse 395] Lancaster County was established on 10 May 1729 out of the western portion of Chester County.

XL. [verse 397] The Manor was a tract of 16,500 acres (more than 25 square miles). "Its borders ran from the mouth of the Conestoga northward along the Susquehanna River." ref. *"The Earth is the Lord's,"* op. cit., p. 196.

XL. [verses 397-398] ref. *"The Earth is the Lord's,"* op. cit., pp. 197-198, 203.

XL. [verse 399] Fifty acres "shall be allotted to a servant, at the end of his service" (ref. Chessman A. Herrick. *"White Servitude in Pennsylvania,"* John Joseph McVey, Philadelphia, 1926, p. 32).
https://archive.org/details/whiteservitudein00herr/page/32

XL. [verse 399] Whereas the Scotch-Irish "were repeatedly ousted from rude cabins they built on the manor," the newly arrived Mennonites promised to pay off their land "within three months" of their surveys. (ref. *"The Earth is the Lord's,"* op. cit., pp. 197, 220).

XL. [verse 400] ref. *"The Earth is the Lord's,"* op. cit., p. 223.

XL. [verse 401] On 14 February 1730, the Scotch-Irish constable John Galbraith of Donegal, under orders from James Logan, "pulled down and destroyed twenty-nine houses and logg buildings" of non-Mennonite squatters within Manor's bounds." It seemed to depend on whether the squatters were Palatine or Scotch-Irish; the Palatines were described as "able to pay." (ref. *"The Earth is the Lord's,"* op. cit., p. 227).

XL. [verse 402] ref. *"The Earth is the Lord's,"* op. cit., pp. 203, 223, 227.

XL. [verse 403] Harrisburg was settled as a trading post by John Harris Sr., a settler from Yorkshire, England, in 1719. A well established Indian trail, known as the Allegheny Path, forded the Susquehanna River at this location. (ref. Paul A. Wallace, *"Historic Indian Paths of Pennsylvania,"* Quarterly Journal of the Historical Society of Pennsylvania, Vol. LXXVI, No. 4, October 1952, p. 433). https://archive.org/details/historicindianpa00wall/page/22 https://journals.psu.edu/pmhb/article/download/31035/30790 -- p. 433.

XL. [verse 404] ref. map of "Landforms of the United States," by Erwin Raisz. https://www.davidrumsey.com/luna/servlet/detail/RUMSEY~8~1~267284~90041658:Landforms-of-the-United-States-

XL. [verses 405-409] ref. Ellen Churchill Semple, "The Appalachian Barrier" and "The Westward Movement," in *"American History and its Geographic Conditions,"* The Riverside Press, Cambridge, Massachusetts, 1903, pp. 38-39, 54-55, 58-59. https://archive.org/details/americanhistoryi00semp https://archive.org/details/americanhistoryi00semp_1

XL. [verse 409] ref. Harrisburg PA (1899) and New Bloomfield PA (1907) USGS 15 minute topographic maps (1:62500).

XL. [verse 410] The Scots-Irish settlement at Middle Spring was three miles downstream from where Shippensburg is today, almost exactly equidistant from Williamsport and Harrisburg. This truly was the middle of nowhere.

XL. [verses 411-412] "A group of Scotch Irish immigrants settled in this area in about 1730. The Scotch-Irish were the earliest settlers on the Pennsylvania frontier" (ref. *"Middle Springs Presbyterian Church,"* at wikipedia.org) These "were immigrants from Ireland and Scotland, and the descendants of those who had taken root in Lancaster County." (ref. *"History of Cumberland County, Pennsylvania,"* Warner, Beers & Co., 1886, Part II, Chapter II, p. 25, at http://www.usgwarchives.net/pa/cumberland/beers/beers.htm

XL. [verse 413] Cumberland County was established on 27 January 1750, from the portion of Lancaster County lying west of the Susquehanna River.

XL. [verse 413] The earliest land records for Cumberland County are online at: http://www.usgwarchives.net/pa/cumberland/land.htm For the earliest list of taxables, ref. *"History of Cumberland County, Pennsylvania,"* op. cit., pp. 11-15. *"Cumberland County, Pennsylvania Quarter Session Dockets 1750-1785"* are online at https://www.ancestry.com/search/collections/flhg-cumberlandcountypaqtrsessdoc

XL. [verse 414] Anderson, Barry, Bruce, Cunningham, Driver, Frazer, Gorden, Grant, Harper, Hood, Hosaic, Hunter, Jack, Johnson, Johnston, Lasey, Levan, Lindsey, Linn, Linton, Martin, McCain, McClean, McDaniel, McIntosh, McKay, Mercer, Moore, Nickels, Price, Reese, Robinson, Robison, Scott, Simpson, Taylor, Wier, Willson.

PART FOUR

XLI. [verse 417] In 1780 the National Methodist Conference in Baltimore officially condemned slavery. (ref. Wikipedia, citing William J. Switala, *"Underground Railroad in Delaware, Maryland, and West Virginia,"* Stackpole Books, Mechanicsburg, Pennsylvania, 2004).

XLI. [verse 419] ref. Sir James Fitzjames Stephen, *"A Digest of the Criminal Law (Crimes and Punishments),"* Fourth Edition, Macmillan and Co., London and New York, 1887, Article 93, Seditious Intention Defined, p. 66. https://archive.org/details/adigestcriminal02stepgoog/page/n7

XLI. [verse 420] The Sedition Act 1661 (13 Car 2 St 1 c 1)

XLI. [verse 420] ref. *"A Digest of the Criminal Law,"* op. cit., Article 91, Seditious Words and Libels, p. 65.

XLI. [verse 421] ref. Seditious Libel, in *"Encyclopedia of the American Constitution"* https://www.encyclopedia.com/politics/encyclopedias-almanacs-transcripts-and-maps/seditious-libel

XLI. [verse 422] ref. *"Charter to William Penn and Laws of the Province of Pennsylvania,"* Lane S. Hart, State Printer, Harrisburg, Pennsylvania, Appendix, Chap. XXVIII, Seditious persons fineable at least twenty shillings, p. 114. https://archive.org/details/chartertowillia00commgoog/page/n125

XLI. [verse 422] "The punishments for this offense were rather steep – up to life imprisonment and/or a fine (Blackstone's Criminal Practice 2010, ¶ B18.9). The earlier punishments were significantly more severe in which perpetrators would have their ears cut off for a first offense and recidivism was punishable by death." ref. Clare Feikert-Ahalt, *"Sedition in England: The Abolition of a Law From a Bygone Era,"* Library of Congress, October 2, 2012. https://blogs.loc.gov/law/2012/10/sedition-in-england-the-abolition-of-a-law-from-a-bygone-era/

XLII. [verses 424-425] ref. "An Act Touching Servants Cloths (sic)," in *"Proceedings and Acts of the General Assembly,"* October 1640 [Volume 1, Image 97], and "An Act for the Repeale of a Clause in an Act made the 23d day of October 1640 . . . Entituled an Act for Servants Clothes," October 1663 [Volume 1, Image 496]. Filed under Codes, Compilations of Laws, Rules and Regulations, at http://aomol.msa.maryland.gov/html/index.html

XLII. [verse 426] ref. "Encyclopedia of Survivors," compiled by comparing "Charles County Master Index" of children without indentures to nine countywide indexes, including "Grantee Index to Deeds," all compiled by the author, in *"The Search for Survivors,"* op. cit.

XLII. [verses 427-428] ref. "Encyclopedia of Survivors," in *"The Search for Survivors,"* op. cit. Self-identification as planters or tradesmen, and recording of marks for cattle, hogs, and horses, are abstracted from court records.

XLIII. [verse 431] ref. *"The Search for Survivors,"* op. cit., pp. 54-55.

XLIII. [verses 432-433] ref. "Survivors who Adopted Orphans and Bastards," in *"The Search for Survivors,"* op. cit., pp. 56-57. There are twenty-seven examples. Edward Kite, Thomas Douglass, Thomas Barron, and Edward Williams were fortunate enough to be taught a trade.

XLIII. [verses 434-436] ref. "Survivors who Rescued Servants Without Indentures," in *"The Search for Survivors,"* op. cit., pp. 58-60.

XLIII. [verse 437] ref. "Encyclopedia of Survivors," in *"The Search for Survivors,"* op. cit., p. 98.

XLIV. [verse 440] ref. "An Act Relateing to Servants and Slaves" in *"Proceedings and Acts of the General Assembly,"* May 1676, Liber W H & L, pp. 102-107 [Volume 2, Image 524]. Filed under Codes, Compilations of Laws, Rules and Regulations, at http://aomol.msa.maryland.gov/html/index.html See also Perpetual Laws of Maryland [19.pdf #169 et seq.]

XLIV. [verse 441] ref. "An Act Relateing to Servants and Slaves," May 1676, op. cit., [Volume 2, Image 524].

XLIV. [verse 443] ref. *"Birth and Shipping Records,"* op. cit., p. 149.

XLIV. [verse 444] ref. *"The Search for Survivors,"* op. cit., pp. 3, 101, citing Charles County Court Records, 8 November 1691 [17.pdf #157].

XLIV. [verse 445] ref. "Encyclopedia of Survivors," in *"The Search for Survivors,"* op. cit., pp. 101-102. Four children of Edward Darnell are identified: Elizabeth, her marke of cattle & hogs, 9 September 1707 [Liber Z, Page 260]; John, gift of livestock, 8 July 1714 [Liber F, Page 17]; Sarah and Thomas, gifts of livestock, 14 December 1726 [Liber L, Page 312].

XLIV. [verses 446-447] On 11 June 1706, Edward Darnall (sic) was indicted for "entertaining" William Mackeboy, "a servant man belonging to Mr. John Smith," for the space of one night. On 10 September 1706, Cornelius White was assigned by the Court to defend Edward Darnell, who was "acquitted and discharged." ref. *"The Search for Survivors,"* op. cit., p. 50, citing Charles County Court Records [23.pdf #122, 142].

The twelve members of the jury are identified by name in the Court Records: Thomas Stone, William Barton, John Mellon, Robert Robinson, Richard Hodgson, Richard Dod, Thomas Coleman, William Watts, William Hardy, Thomas Barron, William Nichols, John Lofton.

XLIV. [verse 448] Mary Williamson, a runaway servant from Virginia, was "conveyed to Thomas Coleman Constable of Benedict Hundred in Charles County." ref. *"The Search for Survivors,"* op. cit., p. 199, citing Charles County Court Records, 14 November 1699 [20.pdf #99]. John Atterberry, servant to Thomas Coleman, confessing to 50 days absence, was sentenced to 500 days servitude. ref. *"The Search for Survivors,"* op. cit., p. 166, citing Charles County Court Records, 13 November 1705 [23.pdf #104].

XLIV. [verse 449] John Loftley alias Lofton embezzled the estate of John Scroggin, an orphan. ref. *"The Search for Survivors,"* op. cit., pp. 381-382, citing Charles County Court Records, 11 June 1700 [21.pdf #10] and 10 November 1702 [22.pdf #64]. And he caused Hugh Davies, "a cripple," to go to Court at least three times for his freedom corn and clothes. ref. *"The Search for Survivors,"* op. cit., pp. 27, 103, citing Charles County Court Records, 13 January 1702 [21.pdf #181], 10 November 1702 [22. pdf #78], and 8 June 1703 [22.pdf #117].

XLIV. [verses 450-451] An arrest warrant was issued against Richard Hodgson for "unlawfully & unreasonable beateing & woundeinge" of his servant Edward Webster. ref. *"The Search for Survivors,"* op. cit., pp. 26, 249, citing Charles County Court Records, 13 January 1680 [09.pdf #143]. Five servants of Richard Hodgson had to petition the Court for their freedom corn and clothes. ref. "Petitions for Freedom," in *"The Search for Survivors,"* op. cit., Margaret Attkinson (p. 203), James Gallaway (p. 214), William Moody (pp. 225-226), Edward Webster (pp. 235-236, Hugh Williams (p. 237). Richard Hodgson his son received John William an "East Indian slave" from "Johannah Hodgson his mother." Although "purchased about fifteen or sixteen years since," and claimed as a servant for life, he was freed by the Court. ref. *"The Search for Survivors,"* op. cit., pp. 37, 237, citing Charles County Court Records, 12 November 1706 [23.pdf #153]and 14 January 1707 [23.pdf #161].

XLIV. [verse 453] William Barton adopted John Hayward, 12 January 1669 [Vol. 60:180], and Martha Smith, 8 November 1692 [17.pdf #277]. Robert Robinson adopted Margret Deveau, 10 March 1713 [25.pdf #120], and Thomas Morris, 12 March 1706 [23.pdf #114]. Richard Dod adopted John Warner and Elizabeth Warner, 27 March 1677 [08.pdf #32]. William Watts adopted Benjamin Cone, 8 August 1704 [23.pdf #20]. William Nichols adopted Rice Jenkins, 12 January 1697 [19.pdf #92], and Susannah Scroggin, 13 August 1700 [11.pdf #19]. ref. "Index to Orphans," in *"The Search for Survivors,"* op. cit., pp. 358, 360, 366, 369, 375, 382, 383, 387.

XLIV. [verse 453] ref. "Vital Records" and "Gifts of Livestock," in *"The Search for Survivors,"* op. cit. William Barton Jr. had five children, two died young (p. 252). Richard Dod had four children, two died young (p. 257). William Nichols had two children (p. 330). No doubt other members of the jury also had children. The Vital Records are fragmentary.

XLV. [verse 455] ref. "Recaptured Runaways," in *"The Search for Survivors,"* op. cit., pp. 166-200.

XLV. [verse 456] John Cooke, John Edgerley, Henry Evers, James Gilbard, Bryan Harrison, John Hawkins, James Hollywood, James Kenneday, Joseph Leman, Elizabeth Powell, Thomas Powell, William Sumerton, Hugh Williams.

XLV. [verses 457-458] ref. Harpers Ferry WV (1893) USGS 30 minute topographic map.

XLV. [verse 462] In 1716, Alexander Spotswood, Lieutenant Governor of Virginia, with a party of 41 persons, crossed the Blue Ridge through Swift Run Gap and followed Elk Run down to the Shenandoah River (ref. Charles E. Kemper, "The Settlement of the Valley," in *Virginia Historical Magazine*, Vol. 30, 1922, p, 171) https://archive.org/details/jstor-4243876/page/n3

Spotswood is usually regarded as the first white man to look upon the Great Valley of Virginia, upon which basis he claimed these lands for the king (ref. Joseph A. Waddell, *"Annals of Augusta County, Virginia, from 1726 to 1871,"* Second Edition, C. Russell Caldwell, Staunton, Virginia, 1902, p. 18). https://archive.org/details/annalsofaugustac00wadd/page/18

Such claims were based upon the "Doctrine of Discovery," from the Papal Bull "Inter Caetera," issued by Pope Alexander VI on 4 May 1493, which stated that any land not inhabited by Christians was available to be "discovered." https://www.gilderlehrman.org/content/doctrine-discovery-1493

The British had no idea that white settlers were living beyond the Blue Ridge.

XLV. [verse 463] ref., for example, J. Lewis Peyton, *"History of Augusta County, Virginia,"* Samuel M. Yost & Son, Staunton, Virginia, 1882, pp. 6-7. https://archive.org/details/historyofaugusta00peytuoft/page/6

XLVI. [verse 464] Robert Barton, Thomas Bayhan, John Berry, Elizabeth Bonner, Stephen Bridges, John Bryan (servant to Thomas Jenkins), Samuell Burgesse, Patrick Cusack, John Cooke, Hugh Davies, James Drunckore, Bryan Farrell, Edward Fo(r)ster, James Gilbard, Argalus Gill, George Gleeve(s), William Gray, Elizabeth Halliburton, William Harris(on), William Herald, James Hollywood, Grace Holmes, Robert Jones (servant to Thomas Hussey), Alexander Killpatrick, James Lackey, James Leech, Edward Lewis, James Low, Margaret Macklanan, Daniell Mahoni, Elizabeth Maybanke, Ellis Morris, John Newton, Thomas Perry, Jeremiah Todd, Walter Toy, Edward Waters, James Welch, John Whitehead, Thomas Wormely.

These names were derived by comparing the list of "**Recaptured Runaways**" (pp. 166-200) with the "**Charles County Master Index**" (pp. 61-86), both in *"The Search for Survivors,"* op. cit.

XLVI. [verse 465] We do not know the ages of indentured servants. But among those without indentures, the youngest recaptured runaway from Charles County, Maryland was William Harris(on), servant to Capt. John Courts, adjudged to be 13 years of age on 13 June 1693 [18.pdf #81], brought to court as a recaptured runaway on 10 August 1697 after 37 days absence [19.pdf #136].

XLVI. [verse 466] James Leech had served 10 years and 8 months, from 8 June 1675 [07.pdf #63] to 9 February 1686 [13.pdf #48]. Thomas Perry had served 11 years and 5 months, from 13 June 1699 [20.pdf #68] to 14 November 1710 [24.pdf #32].

XLVI. [verse 467] Seventeen runaway servants without indentures, brought to Charles County Court within months of their expected dates of freedom, are listed here, with the additional sentences imposed upon them:

Stephen Bridges, 380 days; Patrick Cusack, 230 days; James Drunckore, 1120 days; Argalus Gill, 1000 days; George Gleeve(s), 140 days; William Gray, 320 days; James Hollywood, 710 days; Grace Holmes, 1000 days; Robert Jones, 260 days; James Lackey, 360 days; James Leech, 180 days; Daniell Mahoni, 50 days; Elizabeth Maybanke, 3 years; John Newton, 100 days; Walter Toy, 124 days; Edward Waters, 680 days; John Whitehead, 160 days.

Three runaway servants without indentures were brought to Charles County Court *after* their terms of servitude had expired:

William Herald, adjudged to be 15 years of age, had already served *more* than seven years, from 14 November 1710, and was sentenced to 496 days more [24.pdf #29] to 11 March 1718 [26.pdf #21]. James Low, adjudged to be 14 years of age, had already served *more* than eight years, from 8 August 1699 [20.pdf #79] to 8 June 1708, and was sentenced to 590 days more [23.pdf #253]. Thomas Perry, adjudged to be 11 years of age, had already served *more* than eleven years, from 13 June 1699 [20.pdf #68] to 14 November 1710, and was sentenced to 820 days more [24.pdf #32].

Most of them ran away again. Patrick Cusack, James Drunckore, Argalus Gill, William Gray and Grace Holmes are on the record as having done so (ref. "Recaptured Runaways," in *"The Search for Survivors,"* op. cit.) Stephen Bridges, Patrick Cusack, James Drunckore, George Gleeve(s), William Herald, James Lackey, James Leech, Elizabeth Maybanke, John Newton, Thomas Perry and John Whitehead never appear in the Charles County records again.

XLVI. [verse 468] Samuell Burgesse, ordered to serve Mrs. Elinor Bayne on 11 March 1690 [16.pdf #114], brought to Charles County Court on 10 June 1690, having been absent "severall times," 60 days in all. [17.pdf #18].

XLVI. [verse 469] James Gilbard, ordered to serve Philip Lines on 10 June 1679 [09.pdf #84], brought to Charles County Court on 10 January 1682, having been absent 40 days. [10.pdf #134] James Gilbard was sentenced to 580 days more. He never appears in the Charles County Court records again.

XLVI. [verse 470] Catherine Fletcher, James Gilbard, John Hawkins, Elizabeth Powell, and Thomas Powell, all servants to Philip Lines, all were brought to Charles County Court on 10 January 1682 as recaptured runaways. [10.pdf #134, 135]

XLVI. [verse 471] For example, Nicholas Cole, George Gleeve(s), Matthew Perrie, Ellis Morris, and Charles Grey, all servants to James Neale, were all brought to Charles County Court on 8 June 1686 as recaptured runaways. [13.pdf #117]

XLVII. [verses 473-474] ref. Edward Bland, Abraham Woode, Sackford Brewster & Elias Pennant, *"The Discovery of New Brittaine. Began August 27, Anno Dom. 1650,"* reprinted by J. Sabin and Sons, New York, 1873.
https://archive.org/details/discoveryofnewbr00blan/page/n7

XLVII. [verse 475] Woods River is now known as New River.

XLVII. [verses 476-477] ref. "The Expedition of Batts and Fallam," John Clayton's Transcript, September 1671. Reprinted by Clarence Walworth Alvord and Lee Bidgood, in *"The First Explorations of the Trans-Allegheny Region by the Virginians, 1650-1674,"* Arthur H. Clark Company, Cleveland, Ohio, 1912, pp. 183-205.
https://archive.org/details/firstexploration00alv/page/182

XLVII. [verse 476] ref. Dublin VA (1891) USGS 30 minute topographic map (1:125000).

XLVIII. [verses 478-495] ref. "The journeys of James Needham and Gabriel Arthur in 1673 and 1674 through the piedmont and mountains of North Carolina to establish trade with the Cherokee," contained in a letter from Abraham Wood to John Richards, August 22, 1674. Reprinted in *"The First Explorations of the Trans-Allegheny Region by the Virginians,"* op. cit., pp. 209-227. https://archive.org/details/firstexploration00alv/page/208

XLVIII. [verse 480] The road from Blowing Rock toward Grandfather Mountain still bears the name of "Yonahlossee," a Cherokee word meaning "Trail of the Bear." ref. Cranberry NC (1893) USGS 30 minute topographic map (1:125000).

XLVIII. [verse 481] The ridge across the Nolichucky from Embreeville, where the river bends southwestward, still bears the name of "Cherokee Mountain." ref. Roan Mountain TN 1891 USGS 30 minute quadrangle.

XLVIII. [verse 487] Either the Middle Fork of the Holston to Reed Creek where Wytheville is today, or the South Fork to Cripple Creek. Both routes lead to New River. ref. Wytheville VA (1892) and Hillsville VA (1896) USGS 30 minute topographic maps (1:125000).

XLVIII. [verse 489] ref. Dublin VA (1891), Radford VA (1950), and Pearisburg VA (1932) USGS 15 minute topographic maps (1:62500).

XLVIII. [verse 490] ref. Narrows VA (1932) USGS 15 minute topographic map (1:62500).

XLVIII. [verse 492] ref. Hinton WV (1892) USGS 30 minute (1:125000), and Big Bend WV (1912) USGS 15 minute (1:62500) topographic maps.

XLVIII. [verse 493] ref. Kanawha Falls WV (1901) and Charleston WV (1899) USGS 30 minute topographic maps (1:125000).

XLIX. [verses 496-510] ref. "The journeys of James Needham and Gabriel Arthur in 1673 and 1674," in *The First Explorations of the Trans-Allegheny Region by the Virginians, 1650-1674,* " op. cit.

XLIX. [verse 501] ref. Springdale KY (1935) USGS 15 minute topographic map (1:62500).

XLIX. [verses 502-505] ref. John Filson's 1784 map of Kentucky, available on the Library of Congress website at https://www.loc.gov/item/gm72003144 The general route of the Warrior's Path is shown on the map, and numerous river crossings are identified. Comparison with topographic maps clarifies most of the route.

XLIX. [verses 503-504] Upper Blue Licks, Lulbegrud Creek, and Station Camp Creek are identified by name on John Filson's 1784 map.

XLIX. [verses 504-505] ref. USGS 30 minute topographic maps (1:125000) of Beattyville KY (1892) (Kentucky River crossing is at Irvine), Manchester KY (1891) (Station Camp Creek as shown on the map is the War Fork). and Cumberland Gap KY (1891)

[also available at https://catalog.data.gov/dataset/usgs-1-125000-scale-quadrangle-for-cumberland-gap-ky-1891ebc68]

XLIX. [verses 507-508] ref. *"Atlas to Accompany the Official Records of the Union and Confederate Armies, 1861-1865,"* General Topographical Map, Sheet VII. https://www.loc.gov/resource/g3701sm.gcw0099000/?sp=170 The northern edge shows the route from Cumberland Gap to Moccasin Gap, via Jonesville and Estillville, Virginia. Cherokee Creek, near the bend in the Nolichucky River, is southeast of Jonesborough, Tennessee.

XLIX. [verse 510] ref. Letter from Abraham Wood to John Richards, from Forte Henry, August the 22th, 1674. Endorsed in John Locke's hand. From Public Record Office of London, Shaftesbury Papers, Section IX, Bundle 48, No. 94. "This letter passed into the hands of the Earl of Shaftesbury, whose secretary, John Locke, annotated it." "The original has been carefully compared with Locke's handwriting and it is undoubtedly genuine." https://www.newrivernotes.com/topical_books_1912_virginia_explorationstrans_alleghanyregion.htm This is the same letter transcribed as the preface to "The journeys of Needham and Arthur," in *"The First Explorations of the Trans-Allegheny Region by the Virginians, 1650-1674,"* op. cit.

L. [verses 511, 513] We only have the names of recaptured runaways, not those who actually escaped. But these are persons with a documented history of running away. Most of those who are not found as free adults in the records of Charles County probably ran away again.

L. [verse 511] Only the surnames of male runaways can be traced down through the generations. Of the 280 recaptured runaways not found as free adults in the records of Charles County, 71 (about one-quarter) were women. Only one-eighth of the servants listed in *"Without Indentures,"* op. cit., were women. This suggests that female servants were twice as likely to run away.

L. [verse 512] Elizabeth Hasellton was brought to Charles County Court as a runaway three times in 1667 (see notes for verse 229). Mary Dallyson appeared on 8 June 1680, having run away from Virginia [09.pdf#167]. Two servants who had run away from Charles County (Elizabeth Bonner and James Rouz) appeared on 8 March 1681 [10.pdf #59, 60].

L. [verse 512] Previous acts "haveing hitherto proved ineffectuall," a law was enacted stating "That all and every person or persons apprehending Seizing & takeing upp Such Runnawayes . . . shall have & Receive two hundred pounds of Tobacco" ref. "An Act Relateing to Servants and Slaves" in *"Proceedings and Acts of the General Assembly,"* May 1676, op. cit., [Volume 2, Image 524]. Filed under Codes, Compilations of Laws, Rules and Regulations, at http://aomol.msa.maryland.gov/html/index.html

L. [verse 516] ref. Antietam MD (1938) USGS 15 minute topographic map (1:62500), showing Antietam Creek, where runaways gathered, safely behind the Blue Ridge, beyond the long arm of the law.

L. [verses 517-521]

Maryland State Archives, Maryland Indexes, *"Assessment of 1783,"* Washington County, MSA S 1437
https://msa.maryland.gov/msa/stagser/s1400/s1437/html/1437wa.html

"United States Federal Census," **Washington County, Maryland, 1790,**
https://www.ancestry.com/search/collections/1790usfedcen/

"Maryland, Compiled Marriages, 1655-1850," [Washington County begins 1777], https://www.ancestry.com/search/collections/mdmarriages_ga/

LI. [verse 523] ref. Harpers Ferry WV (1884), Winchester VA (1885), Luray VA (1893), and Woodstock VA (1886) USGS 30 minute topographic maps (1:125000). The forks of the Shenandoah converge at Front Royal, in the northern part of the Luray quadrangle.

LI. [verses 525-527]

"List of Frederick County, Virginia Clerk Fees Belonging to James Wood, Anno Dom. 1744," http://www.usgwarchives.net/copyright.htm

"Marriage Records of Berkeley County, (West) Virginia, 1781-1954,"
https://www.ancestry.com/search/collections/flhg-berkeleyvamarriage/

"West Virginia, Wills and Probate Records, 1724-1985," [Berkeley County begins 1768], https://www.ancestry.com/search/collections/usprobatewv/

"United States Federal Census," Berkeley County, (West) Virginia, 1810
https://www.ancestry.com/search/collections/1810usfedcenancestry/
Note: The 1790 and 1800 federal census records for (West) Virginia are lost.

LI. [verse 528] Last appearances on the record, all within twenty miles of Harpers Ferry, (West) Virginia): Thomas Butterfield, 1810 census, Berkeley County; Jacob Crusin (Crowson), 1810 census, Harpers Ferry, Jefferson County; Henry Underdunk, who married Ann Maddock (31 December 1796), 1820 census, Middletown, Berkeley County; Susannah Varley, who married Ephraim Murphy (17 February 1804), 1860 census, Tomahawk, Berkeley County; Ralph Ware, 1830 census, Shepherds, Jefferson County.

LI. [verse 529] For a vivid description of the Conestoga wagon, ref. Charles Henry Ambler, *"A History of Transportation in the Ohio Valley,"* Arthur H. Clark Company, Glendale, California, 1932, pp. 34-36.

LI. [verses 529-530] The Old National Pike, or Old National Road, was the first major highway built by the federal government. Originally it connected Cumberland, Maryland on the Potomac River with Elizabethtown, Virginia (now Wheeling, West Virginia) on the Ohio River. It was later extended to Vandalia, Illinois along the route of what became U. S. Highway 40.

From Berkeley County, (West) Virginia, along the Old National Pike:

Henry Ingman & Henrietta Rigby migrated to Moores Run, Allegany County, Maryland, twenty miles southwest of Cumberland.

Thomas Varley & Rachel Heaton, and Hugh Lackey & Eleanor Campbell, migrated to Elizabethtown, Ohio County, (West) Virginia, on the Ohio River.

Isaac Bacon & Ruth Siler migrated to Mary Ann Township, Licking County, Ohio, fourteen miles north of the Old National Pike.

After the death of his wife, Henry Ingman migrated to Hocking Township, Fairfield County, Ohio, eighteen miles south of the Old National Pike.

From Berkeley County, via Elizabethtown (Wheeling), along the Ohio River:

John Goddard & Jane Evis migrated to Flemingsburg, Fleming County, Kentucky, seventeen miles from the Ohio River port of Maysville.

Adam Hanshaw & Margaret McKenny migrated to Morganfield, Union County, Kentucky, seven miles from the Ohio River port of Uniontown, seven miles upriver from the Wabash.

For interactive maps of county formation, see https://www.mapofus.org

LII. [verses 532-538] For vivid descriptions of flat boats on the Ohio River, ref. Charles Henry Ambler, *"A History of Transportation in the Ohio Valley,"* op. cit., pp. 41, 49; and Leland D. Baldwin, *"The Keelboat Age on Western Waters,"* University of Pittsburgh Press, 1942, pp. 47-49, 62, 67-72, 77-78.

LII. [verse 535] ref. Clarington OH (1903) USGS 15 minute topographic map (1:62500), 9 to 27 miles downstream from Wheeling.

LIII. [verses 541-542] ref. Ellen Churchill Semple, "Early Trans-Allegheny Settlements," in *"American History and its Geographic Conditions"* op. cit., pp. 77-78.

LIII. [verse 543] ref. Charles E. Kemper, "The Settlement of the Valley," in *Virginia Historical Magazine,* Volume 30, 1922, pp. 169-170. https://archive.org/details/jstor-4243876/page/n1

LIII. [verse 544] ref. Murray N. Rothbard, *"Conceived in Liberty,"* Volume 2, pp. 552-553. https://archive.org/details/ConceivedInLiberty/page/n579

LIII. [verse 545] Scattered far and wide throughout the Shenandoah Valley: Benigar, Coin, Corder, Crookshanks, Crummy, Cusick, Flanagan, Gainer, Goff, Gulley, Jeffries, Kilpatrick, Lackey, Leech, McAvoy, McDonnel, McGraw, McKenny, Motes, Munroe, Rigby, Rowen, Ware (Frederick, Shenandoah, Rockingham, Augusta, and Rockbridge counties).

LIII. [verse 545] Clustered where New River enters into West Virginia: Burdett, Corder, Crouch, Dickins, Flanagan, Goff, Gulley, Jefferies, Kilpatrick, Lackey, Leech, McGraw, Puttuff, Rigby, Rowan, Turley, Whitehead (Montgomery, Botetourt, Monroe, Greenbrier, and Kanawha counties).

LIII. [verse 545] At the Holston River where a trail led to Kentucky: Cusick, Flanagan, Goff, Harrald, Leech, McAvoy, McKenny, McNew, Motes, Rowan, Todd, Turley, Ware, Whitehead (Wythe and Washington counties).

LIII. [verse 547] On the Cumberland River, across from Cherokee: Burdit, Cheston, Collum, Flanagan, Goff, Harrold, Lackey, Leech, Robards, Todd, Turley, Ware, Whitehead (Pulaski, Wayne, Adair, and Cumberland counties).

LIII. [verse 547] On the Warriors' Path, at the Ford of the Kentucky: Crouch, Ellison, Flanagan, Goff, Gulley, Hagan, Lackey, McQueen, Rowin, Todd, Ware (Estill and Madison counties).

LIII. [verse 547] Along the Stoner Creek, or on the Buffalo Trace: Bridges, Crouch, Flanagan, Godard, McKenney, McNew, Ruth, Todd, Turley, Whitehead (Bourbon County).

LIII. [verse 547] On the road to Lexington: Bridges, Collum, Corder, Flanagan, Goff, Hagan, Lackey, McKenney, Robards, Rouse (Clark County).

LIII. [verse 547] On the Logan Trace: Bridges, Burdett, Goff, Greenwood, Gully, Herrald, Jeffries, Kilpatrick, Lackey, Leech, Line, Whitehead (Garrard and Lincoln counties).

LIII. [verses 548-549] ref. "Reaches Crab Orchard," pp. 333-334, and "Itinerant Perils, p. 363, in Ezra Squier Tipple, ed., *"The Heart of Asbury's Journal,"* Eaton & Mains, New York, 1904. https://archive.org/details/heartofasburysjo00asbu/page/n7

LIII. [verse 550] The 1820 census identifies the localities within Lincoln County. The names of Bridges, Goff, Greenwood, Lackey and Leech appear at Crab Orchard, where the Logan Trace emerged onto the bluegrass country. Among them are Mathew, Reuben and Edward Leech, married in Greenbrier County, (West) Virginia in 1795, 1797 and 1799, probably at Petersville (now in Monroe County), near the New River Narrows, where others named Leech can be found in the census records. Reubin Leach (sic) first appears in the records of Kentucky in 1805, when he obtained a land grant for 145 acres on Caney Fork, Buck Creek, Lincoln County. By 1822, Reuben Leech had five land grants for 695 acres, and Mathew Leech had two land grants for 150 acres. William Leech obtained a land grant for 50 acres in 1821, and Edward Leech for 150 acres in 1834, in Lincoln County. ref. *"Kentucky, Land Grants, 1782-1924,"* https://www.ancestry.com/search/collections/kentuclg

LIII. [verses 551-552] ref. Ellen Churchill Semple, **"The Westward Movement,"** in *"American History and its Geographic Conditions,"* op. cit., pp. 73-74.

LIV. [verses 553-554] ref. *"English Folk Songs from the Southern Appalachians,"* Collected by Cecil J. Sharp, Edited by Maud Karpeles, Oxford University Press, London, 1932. Sharp and Karpeles made three visits to the Appalachian Mountains, from 25 July to 28 September 1916, from 11 April to 14 October 1917 (including ten weeks in Kentucky), and from 16 April to 10 October 1918 (pp. xiii-xv). Their itinerary shows them arriving at Pineville Station, Bell County, Kentucky on 25 August 1917, departing on 1 September 1917, visiting Pine Mountain, Harlan County, Kentucky in the interim, and collecting 45 folk songs.

LIV. [verse 555] This area was all part of Lincoln County from 1780 until 1799, and was all part of Knox County until 1818 and 1819, when Whitley and Harlan counties were created. ref. https://www.mapofus.org/kentucky The earliest land records are from 1780 (Lincoln County), 1800 (Knox County), 1816 (Whitley County), and 1820 (Harlan County). The earliest marriage records are from 1792 (filed as Whitley County), 1809 (Knox County), and 1818 (Harlan County). The earliest tax records are from 1800 (Knox County). The earliest census records are from 1810 (Knox County).

LIV. [verses 555-556] "the only secular music" that the hillsman hears "and has, therefore, any opportunity of learning is that which his British forefathers brought with them from their native country and has since survived by oral tradition." (ref. *"English Folk Songs,"* op. cit., p. xxvi)

LIV. [verse 556] "It was . . . in Kentucky that we obtained the best ballad-texts" (ref. *"English Folk Songs,"* op. cit., p. xv).

LIV. [verse 557] "so remote and shut off from outside influence" are "these sequestered mountain valleys" that the speech of the inhabitants "is English, not American, and, from the number of expressions they use which have long been obsolete elsewhere, and the old-fashioned way in which they pronounce many of their words, it is clear that they are talking the language of a past day" (ref. *"English Folk Songs,"* op. cit., p. xxii).

LIV. [verse 558] "I could get what I wanted from pretty nearly everyone I met, young and old." "On one occasion, . . . a small boy tried to edge himself into my cabin . . . and, later on, when my singer failed to remember a song I had asked for, my little visitor came to the rescue and straightway sang the ballad from beginning to end in the true traditional manner" (ref. *"English Folk Songs,"* op. cit., p. xxv).

LIV. [verse 559] "The present inhabitants of the Laurel Country are the direct descendants of the original settlers who were emigrants from England and, I suspect, the lowlands of Scotland." (ref. *"English Folk Songs,"* op. cit., p. xxii) If the pentatonic or hexatonic scale "in the mountain tunes is any indication of the ethnological origin of the singers, it seems to point to the North of England, or to the Lowlands, rather than the Highlands, of Scotland." (ref. *"English Folk Songs,"* op. cit., pp. xxxi-xxxiv)

LIV. [verse 561] ref. Jonesville VA (1891) USGS 30 minute topographic map (1:125000), showing the remote location of Creech, Kentucky, consisting of one cabin, between Pine Mountain and Big Black Mountain, fourteen miles upstream from the Cumberland River. The "Laurel Public Road" led to their cabin (ref. 1910 census, Lower Poor Fork, Harlan County, Kentucky).

LIV. [verses 562-563] Tilford Creech sang one song, "Earl Brand" (No. 4K), to Cecil Sharp and Maud Karpeles, who identify the location and date as "Pine Mountain, Harlan Co., Ky., Aug. 30, 1917." (ref. *"English Folk Songs from the Southern Appalachians,"* op. cit., p. 25) "Earl Brand" was first published in as "The Douglas Tragedy," in Scott's "Minstrelsy of the Scottish Border," 1803. (ref. *"English and Scottish Popular Ballads,"* Volume I, by Francis James Child, Riverside Press, Cambridge, England, 1882, p. 100) https://archive.org/details/englishscottishp11chilrich/page/n11

Tilford Creech (1898-1959) did not learn this song from a book. He had attended school, and he could read and write, as documented in the 1910 census. But his ancestors arrived in America long before "Scott's Minstrelsy" was published. His father's father, William Creech (1845-1918), and his mother's mother, Martha A. Nolen (1860-), were first cousins; both were grandchildren of Enoch Creech (1802-1852) and Susanna "Sally" Blair (1805-1852), who were born in North Carolina and Virginia, respectively, according to the 1850 census. The family appears in the census records for Harlan County from 1820 onward; there are five marriages recorded in 1830, four of them on the same day; and there are fourteen land grants amounting to 940 acres between 1823 and 1829. By the turn of the century the Creech family had been awarded ninety land grants amounting to 9,117 acres, more than fourteen square miles.

The family lived also in Lee County, Virginia, which is contiguous to Harlan County, Kentucky, on the opposite side of Cumberland Mountain. ref. Jonesville VA (1891) USGS topographic map (1:125000). John Creech (died 2 March 1850, Harlan County) is believed to have been Enoch's father. Elijah Creech (born c. 1780) and Jonathan Creech (born c. 1786) are believed to have been John's brothers and Enoch's uncles. According to the 1850 census, both Elijah and Jonathan were born in Virginia. All three brothers are listed in the census for Lee County or Harlan County in 1820, 1830, 1840 and 1850. Previous generations are unconfirmed. Family legend traces the family back to Jamestown in 1622, but the name of Creech does not appear in the lists of settlers in "The Generall Historie of Virginia," 1584-1624. http://docsouth.unc.edu/southlit/smith/smith.html See also www.ancestry.com Message Boards "Jamestown, VA Indian Massacre"

LIV. [verse 564] The earliest record pertaining to America in which I have found the name of Creech is for Middlesex County Court, London, England, 6 August 1661, when William Stone was indicted "for transporting George Creech and Thomas Riddle to America." (ref. "Indictments for Kidnapping," in *"Supplement to the Trilogy,"* op. cit., p. 48).

LV. [verse 569] The four men who signed the Germantown Protest of 1688 were Garret Henderichs, Derick op de graeff, Francis Daniell Pastorius, and Abraham op Den graef. https://kuscholarworks.ku.edu/handle/1808/13386

LV. [verses 570-571] "An Exhortation & Caution to Friends Concerning Buying or Keeping of Negroes," by George Keith, 1693, reprinted by George Moore, ed., "The First Printed Protest Against Slavery in America," in *"The Pennsylvania Magazine of History and Biography,"* Philadelphia, 1889. http://www.qhpress.org/quakerpages/qwhp/gk-as1693.htm

LV. [verse 572] The first children without indentures in the surviving records of Pennsylvania appeared in Chester County Court on 3 October 1693.

LV. [verse 572] In Pennsylvania, children without indentures were to serve until the age of twenty-one, unless otherwise specified by the Court. The last were brought to Chester County Court in 1697, the youngest being ten years of age, who would serve until 1708. Four in nearby counties would not be free until somewhat later. Richard Cundon, age twelve, was brought to Kent County Court in 1700 and would serve until 1709. Robert Barry, age ten, was brought to Bucks County Court in 1699 and would serve until 1710. John Anderson and Daniel MacCay, "of Ireland," age ten and eleven, were brought to Burlington County Court in 1700 and would serve until 1711 and 1710, respectively. (ref. *"Supplement to the Trilogy,"* op. cit., pp. 69-77).

LV. [verse 573] ref. "Negro Import Duties in Colonial Pennsylvania," by Darold D. Wax, in *"The Pennsylvania Magazine of History and Biography,"* Vol. 97, No. 1, January 1973, pp. 22-24.

LV. [verse 573] ref. "An Impost Act, Laying a Duty on Negroes, Wine, Rum and Other Spirits, Cider and Vessels," in *"The Statutes at Large of Pennsylvania,"* 1710-1711, Chapter CLXXXI, pp. 382-388, end notes.

LV. [verse 575] James Boareman, John Glover, Mollatto Will, and Thomas Fountain. ref. *"The Search for Survivors,"* op. cit., pp. 39-40.

LVI. [verses 577-585] ref. *"The Search for Survivors,"* op. cit., pp. xxvi, 45, citing Charles County Court Records, 8 August 1732 [32.pdf #100].

PART FIVE

LVII. [verse 588] Nearly the entire route of the highway from Williamsburg, Virginia to Boston, Massachusetts may be viewed online, in segments.

The King's Highway from "Williamsbourg," via "Frederi(ck)sbourg," to "Belhaven or Alexandrie" on the Potomac River:
https://www.loc.gov/resource/g3880.ar143700/?r=0.166,0.267,0.646,0.357,0

Old Baltimore Pike from Alexandria, via Annapolis and Baltimore, to New Castle on the Delaware River:
https://www.loc.gov/resource/g3840.ct001244/

Old Philadelphia Road from Newcastle, via Philadelphia and Bristol, to Trenton on the Delaware River:
https://collections.leventhalmap.org/search/commonwealth:6t053q304

Old Post Road from Trenton, via Brunswick, to Woodbridge
https://www.loc.gov/resource/g3810.ar124101/

Boston Post Road from New York, via New Haven and New London, to Boston
upload.wikimedia.org/wikipedia/commons/e/e7/Boston_Post_Road_map.png

LVII. [verses 590-592] James Hambleton, born c. 1682 (ref. "Berwick, Maine, and Nova Scotia Hamiltons," by Rev. Arthur Wentworth Hamilton Eaton, in *"The New England Historical and Genealogical Register,"* Volume XLIV, Boston, 1890, pp. 361-365), was "adjudged to be twelve yeares of age" and "ordered to serve according to law," that is, for twelve years, until the age of twenty-four (ref. Westmoreland County, Virginia, Order Book, 26 April 1699). Had he been adjudged to be sixteen years of age, he would have served five years. He was the son of David Hambleton of Westburn, Lanarkshire, Scotland, "captured by Oliver Cromwell at the Battle of Worcester, England, September 3, 1651; brought to America as a prisoner in chains on the *John and Sarah* in the same year" (ref. historical marker at the junction of Sligo Road and Pinch Hill Road, Rollinsford, New Hampshire). James Hambleton was sentenced to five months for running away, one year for violently assaulting his master "on the Queen's Road," and twenty lashes for his "arrogant and saucy words and behavior" before the court (ref. Westmoreland County, Virginia, Order Book, 26 March 1707). He was not freed by the court until 24 February 1714. He and his wife Grace died in Westmoreland County, Virginia, and three children are named in their wills (Deeds and Wills, 15 April 1727 and 18 April 1727).

LVIII. [verse 593] Twenty-eight children without indentures found in the court records of Maryland or Virginia have been identified with a high degree of certainty in Massachusetts, both in the birth records and as grown adults after their expected dates of freedom. None came from anywhere north of Gloucester, Massachusetts, and none were in servitude anywhere south of York County, Virginia (ref. "Kids from Massachusetts," in *"Birth and Shipping Records,"* op. cit., pp. 253-264). Today the distance between Yorktown and Gloucester is 630 to 650 miles, depending upon the route traveled.

LVIII. [verses 594-595] ref. *"Birth and Shipping Records,"* op. cit., p. 254.

LVIII. [verse 596] ref. "Index to Ship Captains," revised, in *"Supplement to the Trilogy,"* op. cit., pp. 52-57.

LVIII. [verse 597] "Administration of estate of Mr. John Huberd, dec'd, is granted to Katherine Huberd, his relict. Estate is to be appraised by Mr. John Page, Mr. Otho Thorpe, Mr. James Besouth and Mr. William Newman." (ref. *"York County, Virginia Records 1665-1672,"* abstracted and compiled by Benjamin B. Weisiger III, p. 90 et seq.)

LVIII. [verse 598] ref. "Profiles of Child Traffickers," in *"Birth and Shipping Records,"* op. cit., pp. 25-26, 30.

LVIII. [verse 599] ref. *"Without Indentures,"* op. cit., pp. 224-227. John Huberd is identified as the brother of Mathew Huberd in a Power of Attorney by Sibella Huberd, relict of Mr. Mathew Huberd, dated 22 July 1667 (ref. *"York County, Virginia Records 1665-1672,"* op. cit., p. 80).

LVIII. [verse 600] John Bray was adjudged to be fifteen years of age on 24 January 1668. Under Virginia law he would serve until the age of twenty-four. (ref. *"Without Indentures,"* op. cit., p. x, citing Hening, *"Statutes at Large; Virginia,"* op. cit., March 1661-2, Act XCVIII) His expected date of freedom was 1677. Under Virginia law, prior to 1705, it was merely a "laudable custom" to allow servants corn and clothes at the expiration of their terms of service. Nothing was mandatory for the master to provide. (ref. *"Without Indentures,"* op. cit., pp. xv)

LVIII. [verse 604] ref. *"Massachusetts Town and Vital Records Collection, 1620-1988,"* compiled by New England Historic Genealogical Society, Boston, Massachusetts https://www.ancestry.com/search/collections/matownvital

LVIII. [verse 605] "Tho: Bray of Glocester ship carpenter married to Marie Wilson of the same towne," 3 March 1646

LIX. [verse 607] ref. *"A Genealogical Memoir of the Lo-Lathrop Family in This Country,"* by Rev. E. B. Huntington, Published by Mrs. Julia M. Huntington, Ridgefield, Connecticut, 1884, pp. 24-25
https://archive.org/details/genealogicalmemo00byuhunt/page/24

LIX. [verse 608] During the months that Rev. John Lothrop was imprisoned in "The Clink," "His wife fell sick, of which sickness she died." (ref. *"A Genealogical Memoir,"* op. cit., p. 25) It is said that her maiden name was Hannah House, and that she was the older sister of Samuel House (Baptized 10 June 1610, Eastwell, Kent, England), who moved in 1645 to Barnstable, Massachusetts, where Rev. Lothrop had established a new community and built a church. http://jtbullock.com/Tree/BenSitton.html#SH

LIX. [verse 609] "Samuel Howse of Scituat shipwright," letter of attorney to Tho: Tarte, 20 July 1649. http://jtbullock.com/Tree/BenSitton.html#SH

LIX. [verse 609] "John Sutton junior of Cittuate in New England Carpinter," stated in a deed dated 1653, Suffolk County, Massachusetts. His descendants believe he was a ship carpenter.
http://huskey-ogle-family.tripod.com/ancestorarchives/id46.html

LIX. [verse 610] ref. "Kids from Massachusetts," in *"Birth and Shipping Records,"* op. cit., p. 261.

LIX. [verse 611] John Sutton was adjudged to be seventeen years of age on 18 November 1679. Under Maryland law he would serve for seven years. His expected date of freedom was 1686. (ref. *"Without Indentures,"* op. cit, p. 11, citing *"Proceedings and Acts of the General Assembly,"* op. cit., April 1666 – June 1676, " Volume 2, p. 335, October 1671)

LIX. [verses 611-612] John House was brought to court on 7 April 1686. John Sutton would not have been free until 18 November 1686. By the time he returned to Massachusetts, his cousin was already missing.

LIX. [verse 612] ref. "Kids from Massachusetts," in *"Birth and Shipping Records,"* op. cit., p. 258.

LX. [verse 614] "Deacon John Pearson (1610-1693) and wife Dorcas came from England to Ipswich, then to Rowley, Mass., in 1643.
(ref. www.findagrave.com)

"Jeremy Pearson, son of John & Dorcas, borne the eight moneth the twenty fift day," Anno 1653. Rowley, Massachusetts (ref. *"Massachusetts Town and Vital Records Collection,* op. cit.)

"Jno. Pearson, son of Jeramiah & Prissilla, borne the tenth of Aprill 1690," Rowley, Massachusetts (ref. *"Massachusetts Town and Vital Records Collection,* op. cit.)

LX. [verses 615-616] "John Pearson, son of Lieutenant Jeremiah and Priscilla Pearson, who inherited the mills from his father, had a most interesting career early in life. He ran away to sea at the age of twelve and visited the West Indies. Tradition says that he narrowly escaped capture by pirates, although nothing has been found to substantiate this." (ref. "The Pearsons and their Mills," by Russell Leigh Jackson, in *"The Essex Institute Historical Collections,"* Vol. LXI, October 1925, p. 350)
https://archive.org/details/essexinstitutehi61esse/page/n445

LX. [verse 617] ref. *"Without Indentures,"* op. cit., p. 233, citing Henrico County, Virginia, Order Book & Wills, 12 July 1699.

LX. [verse 618] ref. *"Without Indentures,"* op. cit., p. xv, citing Hening, *"Statutes at Large; Virginia,"* op. cit., October 1705, Act XIII. Freedom dues.

LX. [verse 620] The Boston Post Road passed right through Stonington, Connecticut.
upload.wikimedia.org/wikipedia/commons/e/e7/Boston_Post_Road_map.png

LX. [verse 621] "John Pearson & Elizabeth Mix were married March 24th 1714 by Nathaniel Cheesenbrough, Justice of the Peace. Entered in Stonington, second book of marriages" (Transcribed in records for Newbury, Massachusetts, ref. *"Massachusetts Town and Vital Records Collection,* op. cit.)

LX. [verse 622] "Elizabeth Mix Pearson died at the Pearson house, February 14, 1726 (ref. "The Pearsons and their Mills," op. cit., p. 352). John Pearson is said to have died 26 February 1781, although I cannot confirm this.
http://trees.wmgs.org/familygroup.php?familyID=F22217&tree=Schirado

LX. [verse 623] ref. "Index to Revolutionaries," in *"The Search for Survivors,"* op. cit., pp. 285, 286; and *"Reminiscences of a Nonagenarian,"* by Sarah Anna Emery, ed., William H. Huse & Co., Newburyport, Massachusetts, 1879. p. 173. https://archive.org/details/reminiscencesan00emergoog/page/n186

LXI. [verse 627] Thomas Huit or Hewett was born 23 June 1667 (ref. *"Massachusetts Town and Vital Records Collection,* op. cit.) His father, Ephraim Huit, died 6 May 1678. His mother, Elizabeth Foster, died 15 February 1682/3. All in Hingham, Massachusetts (ref. *"History of the Town of Hingham, Massachusetts,"* Volume II, pp. 358-359, and Volume III, pp. 123-124). https://archive.org/details/historyoftownofh0203hing/page/n5

LXI. [verse 628] "Thomas Taylor presenting to the Court Thomas Hewet his Servant to have Inspection into his age, is (by and with the consent of the said Servant), ordered to serve his said Master or assignes the full time of Seaven years, he the said Taylor declaring in open Court that he will teach him to Read and Right a good leighable hand" (ref. Old Rappahannock County, Virginia, Order Book, 5 March 1683)

LXI. [verses 630-631] Last Will and Testament of Thomas Taylor, probated 2 March 1686/7 (ref. Wills of Old Rappahannock County, Virginia)

LXI. [verse 632] "an unfortunate insane young man," 1689-90 (ref. *"History of the Town of Hingham, Massachusetts,"* op. cit., Volume II, p. 359).

LXII. [verses 633-635] Lieut. James Smith (1645-1690), of Newbury, Mass., "who deceased Nov. 1, 1690, being castaway on Cape Breton on the Canada Expedition." (ref. Essex Co. Hist. Collection, Vol. V., reprinted in *"Society of Colonial Wars in the State of Wisconsin,"* Burdick & Allen, Milwaukee, 1906, p. 116) https://archive.org/details/listofofficersme00gene/page/116
See also: https://en.wikipedia.org/wiki/Battle_of_Quebec_(1690)

LXII. [verses 635-637] ref. "Kids from Massachusetts," in *"Birth and Shipping Records,"* op. cit., p. 261.

LXII. [verse 638] There are fourteen deeds to William Dent dated 10 April 1685 to 10 June 1704, amounting to six thousand acres (ref. "Grantee Index to Deeds," in *"The Search for Survivors,"* op. cit., pp. 297-298.

LXII. [verse 638] ref. Colonel William Dent, in *"The Dents of Friendship,"* Historical Society of Charles County, La Plata, Maryland.
https://charlescountyhistorical.org/html/the_dents_of_friendship.html

LXII. [verse 639] ref. *"The Search for Survivors,"* op. cit., p. 64, citing Charles County Court Records, 19 April 1698 [19.pdf #296].

LXII. [verses 639-642] ref. *"The Search for Survivors,"* op. cit., pp. 240-241, citing Charles County Court Records, 13 June 1699 [20.pdf #68] and 12 September 1699 [20.pdf #90].

LXII. [verse 643] ref. "Kids from London," in *"Birth and Shipping Records,"* op. cit., p. 161.

LXII. [verse 644] "Maj. William Dent brings his Servant Turlough Obryan who desires with ye Approbation of this Court to bargaine with his said Master: That in Consideration that his Master will give his Consent that hee may marry with one Frances Hogg a servant Woman of ye said Maj. Dent, that they will each of them serve ye said Maj. Dent Two whole years upon which agreement they are both to be free, ye fourteenth Day of November in ye yeare 1705: and Maj. Dent promises to Release ye rest of ye said Frances Hoggs service" ref. Charles County Court Records, 14 September 1703 [22.pdf #129] This is the only such entry in seventy-six years of court records in Charles County (1658-1734).

Indentured servants could not marry or have children while under contract. So far as I know, the same was true of servants without indentures. My own ancestor, James Hambleton, was married and had three children while still a servant. Presumably he had verbal permission from his master. There may have been other such cases. In the case of Turlough O'Bryan and Frances Hogg, their court ordered terms of servitude were being changed by mutual agreement, which required approval by the Court.

LXII. [verse 647] Benjamin Smith died 14 May 1723, and has a gravestone in Sawyer Hill Burying Ground, Newbury, Essex County. Massachusetts. https://www.findagrave.com/memorial/100863310

LXII. [verse 648] ref. "Index to Revolutionaries," in *"Birth and Shipping Records,"* op. cit., pp. 269, 274, 275, 298, 299.

LXIII. [verse 649] "Izabel Daughter of Patrick & Mary Hey born August 31 1691," Charlestown, Massachusetts (ref. *"Massachusetts Town and Vital Records Collection,"* op. cit.)

"Here lyes Buried the Body of Mr. Peter Hay, who Departed this Life, April 1st Anno Dom. 1748, in ye 91st Year of His Age." (ref. "Inscriptions in Stoneham Cemetery," in *"New England Historical and Genealogical Register,"* Volume 12, p. 308). Said to be one and the same person as Patrick Hey, born in Scotland.

The old parish registers of Scotland list no Peter Hay (or Hey) born in this time frame. By far the closest match with no marriage on the record is Patrick Hay, son of George Hay, Baptized 26 February 1655, Errol, Perthshire, Scotland. https://www.scotlandspeople.gov.uk

LXIII. [verse 650] "Mary Hey, wife of Patrick Hey, nigh Reding, dyed March 12th 1693/4," Charlestown, Massachusetts (ref. *"Massachusetts Town and Vital Records Collection,"* op. cit.)

LXIII. [verses 651-653] "Mullinax Rattcliffe presents a woman servant named Isabella Hayes to the Court... who is adjudged to be twenty years of age." ref. Charles County Court Records, 8 June 1708 [23.pdf #253] Under Maryland law, she would serve for six years. Her expected date of freedom was 1714. (ref. *"Proceedings and Acts of the General Assembly,"* op. cit., April 1666 – June 1676, " Volume 2, p. 335, October 1671)

LXIII. [verse 654] Today the distance between Port Tobacco and Charlestown is about 500 miles.

LXIII. [verses 655-656] "for the future there shall be nothing allowed to any Servant att the end or Expiracon of his or their Service more than their Clothes, Howes, Axe & Corne" (ref. *"Without Indentures,"* op. cit., p. 15, citing *"Proceedings and Acts of the General Assembly, January 1637/8-September 1664,"* Volume 1, Page 496, Sept.-Oct. 1663). The clothing is frequently described in "Petitions for Freedom," in *"The Search for Survivors,"* op. cit., pp. 214, 220, 221, 229, 230, 234, 236, 237.

LXIII. [verse 658] "Nathaniel Nichols of Reading & Isable Hay of Charlestown were married . . . at Reading, Sept. 26, 1715" (ref. *"Massachusetts Town and Vital Records Collection,"* op. cit.)

LXIII. [verse 659] Based upon the birth records of their children, they moved from Reading to Framingham between 6 March 1719 and 6 April 1727. (ref. *"Massachusetts Town and Vital Records Collection,"* op. cit.)

LXIII. [verse 660] ref. "Index to Revolutionaries," in *"Birth and Shipping Records,"* op. cit., pp. 271, 273, 283, 284.

LXIII. [verse 661] ref. "A Muster roll of Capt. Eaton's Compy. in Col. Green's Regt.," Lexington Alarms, XII, 93, in *"The Battle of April 19, 1775, in Lexington, Concord, Lincoln, Arlington, Cambridge, Somerville and Charlestown, Massachusetts,"* Special Limited Edition, with the Muster Rolls of the Participating American Companies, by Frank Warren Coburn, 1912, pp. 22-23. https://archive.org/details/battleofapril19100cobu/page/n7

LXIII. [verse 662] ref. "A Muster Roll of Cap. John Bachellers Company of Minute men in Colo. Ebenezer Bridges Regt." Lexington Alarms, XI, 245, in *"The Battle of April 19, 1775,"* op. cit., pp. 21-22.

LXIII. [verse 662] https://en.wikipedia.org/wiki/Joseph_Damon_House

Thomas Damon was second cousin to Jason Damon, also a Revolutionary soldier (https://www.findagrave.com/memorial/89446094/jason-damon) The actor and screenwriter Matt Damon is a direct descendant of Jason Damon.

LXIV. [verse 665] "Thomas Walkup the son of George Walkup and Neomy his wife was Born the 16 Day of March Anno 1689," Framingham, Massachusetts (ref. *"Massachusetts Town and Vital Records Collection,"* op. cit.) His mother, Naomi Stevenson, was born 1660 in Massachusetts (ref. *"American Genealogical-Biographical Index"*). According to living descendants, his father was born in Scotland. (ref. *"Birth and Shipping Records,"* op. cit., pp. vii-viii) A search of the old parish records reveals that the surname was spelled Wauchop or Wauchope. The two closest matches are George Wauchope, son of Andrew Wauchope and Margaret Gilmour, Baptized 14 November 1664, Liberton, Midlothian, Scotland, thought to have died young (*"Scottish Surnames: A Contribution to Genealogy,"* by James Paterson, p. 39); and George Wauchope, son of William Wauchope and Grissell Henderson, Baptized 12 February 1664, Edinburgh, Midlothian, Scotland (almost surely the one, as Thomas Walkup had a nephew named Henderson Walkup, Born 4 September 1735, ref. *"Massachusetts Town and Vital Records Collection,"* op. cit.) No other George Wauchope is within twelve years of Naomi's age.

LXIV. [verses 666-667] "Thomas Walcupp servant to Joseph Venables . . . is by the Court adjudged to be Nine Years of Age and Ordered he serve his said Master according to Law." (ref. Northumberland County Virginia Court Order Books, 20 July 1698)

LXIV. [verse 670] Under Virginia law he would serve until the age of twenty-four. (ref. *"Without Indentures,"* op. cit., p. x, citing Hening, *"Statutes at Large; Virginia,"* op. cit., March 1661-2, Act XCVIII)

LXIV. [verse 671] ref. *"Birth and Shipping Records,"* op. cit., pp. vii-viii.

LXIV. [verse 672] Thomas Walkup's expected date of freedom was July 1713. His first child was born 19 June 1717. (ref. *"Massachusetts Town and Vital Records Collection,"* op. cit.)

LXIV. [verse 673] There were six children born to Thomas and Hannah Walkup of Framingham, Massachusetts. The youngest, Thomas Junior, was born 11 September 1727 (ref. *"Massachusetts Town and Vital Records Collection,"* op. cit.) Their marriage record has not survived.

LXIV. [verse 674] ref. *"History of Framingham, Massachusetts, Early Known as Danforth's Farms, 1640-1880, with a Genealogical Register,"* by J. H. Temple, 1887, pp. 217, 218.
https://archive.org/details/historyofframinged00temp/page/n7

LXIV. [verse 675] Estate of Thomas Walkup, Framingham, probated 1755. ref. *Middlesex County, Massachusetts Probate Index, 1648-1870*

LXIV. [verse 676] "Walkup, Francis, s. Thomas, bap. May 26, 1754," ref. "Marlborough Births," in *"Vital Records of Marlborough, Massachusetts,"* Franklin P. Rice, Worcester, 1908, p. 186.

LXIV. [verse 677] ref. *"History of Framingham, Massachusetts,"* op. cit., pp. 226-227. https://archive.org/details/historyofframinged00temp/page/n7

Also *"History of the Town of Marlborough, Middlesex County, Massachusetts, from its First Settlement in 1657 to 1861,"* by Charles Hudson, T. R. Marvin & Son, Boston, 1862, pp. 136, 140. "marched to the relief of Fort William Henry"
https://archive.org/details/historyoftownofm00huds_0/page/n9

LXIV. [verse 679] ref. *History of the Town of Marlborough,"* op. cit., pp. 168-169. https://archive.org/details/historyoftownofm00huds_0/page/n9

LXIV. [verse 681] ref. *History of the Town of Marlborough,"* op. cit., pp. 166-167. https://archive.org/details/historyoftownofm00huds_0/page/n9

LXIV. [verse 682] ref. "Index to Revolutionaries," in *"Birth and Shipping Records,"* op. cit., pp. 283, 285, 290, 295. See also seven additions to the list in *"Supplement to the Trilogy,"* op. cit., p. 67.

LXV. [verse 684] "Thomas sonne of Tho: Wheeler and Hana his wife borne 1 Janr. 1659," Concord, Massachusetts. (ref. *"Massachusetts Town and Vital Records Collection,"* op. cit.)

LXV. [verse 685] "Jno. Wallop's servant boys were brought to court: Munsly Farsy was judged to be 10 years old. Tho, Wheeler was judged to be 18 years old. They were ordered to serve accordingly." (ref. Accomack County, Virginia Court Orders, 18 April 1676)

LXV. [verse 685] For USGS topographic map of Wallops Island, ref. https://www.topozone.com/virginia/accomack-va/island/wallops-island/

LXV. [verse 686] ref. Last Will and Testament of John Wallop, dated 4 April 1693. http://espl-genealogy.org/MilesFiles/site/p567.htm#i56629 He owned 2385 acres on "Gingoteage Creek on the main land of Accomack County," and 2500 acres on "Keeckotanck Island on the seaboard side." (not 7000 acres as stated in the epic poem) Wallops Island was "originally known as Kegotank Island." (ref. https://en.wikipedia.org/wiki/Wallops_Island)

LXV. [verse 686] John Wallop owned five children, whom he brought to Court on 10 September 1674, 16 April 1675, 18 April 1676 and 2 August 1680. He was one of the Gentleman Justices on 2 August 1680 when his own "servant boy," William Dixson, was sentenced to seven years of slavery.

LXV. [verse 687] "Weyley, Timothy, s. of John, (born) Apr. 24, 1653." Reading, Mass. (ref. *"Massachusetts Town and Vital Records Collection,"* op. cit.)

LXV. [verse 687] "Wiley, Elizabeth, w. John, (died) Aug. 3, 1662." Reading, Mass. (ref. *"Massachusetts Vital Records to 1850,"* www.americanancestors.org)

LXV. [verse 688] "Nich: Holmes Brought his Servt Timothy Whaley to have Judgmt of this Courtt for his time who is Ajudgd to serve Six years." ref. Talbot County, Maryland Judgment Record, 21 July 1668 (Archives of Maryland Online, Volume 54, Page 424)

LXV. [verse 688] Reed's Creek Farm, 800 acres, was patented to Thomas Reed in 1659, and later sold to Nicholas Holmes, in whose family it remained until 1765. (ref. https://mht.maryland.gov/secure/medusa/PDF/Talbot/T-314.pdf) Reed Creek, where the Choptank opens to the Chesapeake, is shown on the Oxford MD (1904) USGS 15 minute topographic map (1:62500).

LXV. [verse 689] "William Hagar sonn of William & Mary Hagar borne the 12 of February 1658," Watertown, Massachusetts. (ref. *"Massachusetts Town and Vital Records Collection,"* op. cit.)

LXV. [verse 689] Tho: Baker prsents a Servant to be judged of / Wm Hagar is judged to be 14 yeares old" Ref. Charles County Court Records, 13 April 1669 (Archives of Maryland Online, Volume 60, Page 188) Under Maryland law, William Hagar Jr, would have served seven years.

LXV. [verse 690] William Hagar Jr. of Watertown was impressed into service in Capt. Davenport's company in King Philip's War, according to a muster roll "dated from Nov. 25 to Dec. 3, 1675." (ref. *"Soldiers in King Philip's War: Containing the Lists of the Soldiers of Massachusetts Colony, Who Served in the Indian War of 1675-1677,"* by George Madison Bodge, Boston, 1891, pp. 123-124. https://archive.org/details/soldiersinkingp00bodggoog/page/n154

LXV. [verse 690] Masters and owners had to bring their servants to Court to have their ages adjudged "at or before the third Court in their respective Counties." (ref. *"Proceedings and Acts of the General Assembly, January 1637/8-September 1664,"* Volume 1, Page 352, October 1654). The three preceding sessions commenced 11 August 1668, 8 September 1668 and 12 January 1669. William Hagar Jr. could have served seven years in Maryland before being impressed into service in Massachusetts.

LXV. [verse 692] ref. "Index to Revolutionaries," in *"Birth and Shipping Records,"* op. cit., pp. 267, 269, 276, 277, 278, 282, 286, 287, 290, 291, 297. See additions to the list in *"Supplement to the Trilogy,"* op. cit., p. 67.

LXVI. [verse 693] ref. *"The Battle of April 19, 1775,"* op. cit., pp. 19-20. https://archive.org/details/battleofapril19100cobu/page/n7

LXVI. [verses 693-695] ibid., pp. 23-25.

LXVI. [verses 693-695] ibid., pp. 32-34, 43-46.

LXVI. [verses 696-699] ibid., pp. 60-70.

LXVII. [verses 700-701] ibid., pp. 17-19, 25-27, 37-43.

LXVII. [verse 702] ibid., pp. 78-81.

LXVII. [verse 703] ibid., pp. 81-84.

LXVII. [verse 704] Musicians traditionally wore the opposite colors from the other soldiers in their units "so that the commander could easily grab them in the confusion and smoke of battle and get a signal out to the troops. It was also considered proper battlefield etiquette not to shoot the musician — though a lot of times it happened anyway." (ref. *"Fife & Drum Corps: Old Uniforms, Modern Mission,"* by Michael Lewis) https://www.bands.army.mil/organizations/pages/default.asp?unit=OGFDC&p=news&NewsID=983

LXVII. [verse 705] ref. *"The Battle of April 19, 1775,"* op. cit., pp. 84-85.

LXVII. [verse 706] ibid., pp. 93-94.

LXVII. [verse 707] ref. Concord MA (1943) USGS 15 minute topographic map (1:62500).

LXVII. [verse 708] ref. *"The Battle of April 19, 1775,"* op. cit., p. 90.

LXVII. [verse 709] ibid., pp. 95-99, 109.

LXVII. [verses 711-713] ref. "Index to Revolutionaries," in *"Birth and Shipping Records,"* op. cit., pp. 267, 269, 273, 274, 275, 276, 277, 278, 282, 283, 286, 287, 290, 291, 295, 297, 298, 299. See also *"Supplement to the Trilogy,"* op. cit., p. 67. If active on day one, 19 April 1775, it is noted in the index.

LXVII. [verse [714] At Concord Bridge: From *Concord*, David Brown's Company, Nathan Flint Jr., Daniel Heald (unlisted). From *Acton*, Samuel Reed's Company, Daniel Fletcher, Peter Fletcher; Reuben Butterfield's Company, Jonathan Fletcher; James Burt's Company, Abijah Read (unlisted).

Also engaged at Concord Bridge were: From *Lincoln*, William Smith's Company, Daniel Billing, who later married Lydia Wheeler; and from *Acton*, Isaac Davis' Company, Ebenezer Edwards, who later married Lucy Wheeler; both were great-granddaughters of Thomas Wheeler.

At Meriam's Corner: From *Waltham*, Abraham Pierce's Company, Benjamin Hager, Isaac Hager, Jonathan Hager, William Hager Jr., Josiah Hastings, John Sanderson. From *Woburn*, Joshua Walker's Company, Abel Wyman, Joseph Wyman. From *Chelmsford*, Moses Parker's Company, Charles Fletcher. From *Reading*, Thomas Eaton's Company, Joseph Bancroft, Jonathan Nichols; John Bacheller's Company, Thomas Damon, Timothy Wiley; John Walton's Company, John Hawkes, Isaac Smith Jr., Nathaniel Wiley Sr., Thomas Hudson; John Flint's Company, Henry Putnam. From *Framingham*, Jesse Emes' Company, Thaddeus Hager.

Also engaged at Meriam's Corner were: From *Westford*, Joshua Parker's Company, Calvin Blanchard, who later married Abigail Reed, twin great-granddaughter of Thomas Wheeler. (Calvin was brother of Luther Blanchard, fifer, from *Acton*, Isaac Davis' Company, the first casualty at Concord Bridge). From *Westford*, Oliver Bates' Company, Jonas Holden, who later married Sarah Reed, twin great-granddaughter of Thomas Wheeler. From *Westford*, Jonathan Minot's Company, Elijah Hildreth, who later married Molly Reed, sister of Abigail and Sarah, great-granddaughter of Thomas Wheeler.

Ref. "Index to Muster Rolls," in *"The Battle of April 19, 1775,"* op. cit., pp. 77-78. The muster rolls are indexed by town and commander, at the end of the second part, the very back of the book.
https://archive.org/details/battleofapril19100cobu/page/77

LXVII. [verse 715] Daniel Fletcher, Born 18 October 1718, Acton MA, and Jonathan Nichols, Born 18 June 1758, Reading MA.

LXVIII. [verse 717] Amos Heald, son of Daniel Heald and Abigail Wheeler, Born 18 November 1767, Lincoln MA, Died 5 March 1849, Chester VT. (ref. www.findagrave.com) He was the great-grandson of Thomas Wheeler Sr. (see additions to "Index to Revolutionaries," in *"Supplement to the Trilogy,"* p. 67).

LXVIII. [verse 717] Amos Heald "was with his mother on the hill at Concord and witnessed the battle at Concord Bridge, being about seven years of age" (ref. *"Ancestry, Family History and Relics,"* by Charles Thadeus Heald, 1902). "His father was in the battle. They had a farm above the North Bridge near the Buttricks." (Larry A. Heald, personal communication, 31 December 2018) This would place their vantage point about 300 yards from the west end of the North Bridge at Concord. (ref. *"Map of Middlesex County, Massachusetts,"* by Henry F. Walling, Boston, 1856. The Buttrick house is shown on the map). https://collections.leventhalmap.org/search/commonwealth:1257bb45s#

LXVIII. [verse 718] Daniel Heald, Born 14 July 1739, Concord MA, Died 17 September 1833, Chester VT. (ref. www.findagrave.com) Daniel Heald was no doubt in David Brown's Company, the same as Nathan Flint Jr., a near neighbor. The Flint house was one quarter mile from the North Bridge (ref. *"Map of Middlesex County, Massachusetts,"* op. cit.)

LXVIII. [verses 719-720] Relations to Abigail Wheeler Heald: Daniel Fletcher was her first cousin's husband. Peter Fletcher, Jonathan Fletcher, and Abijah Reed were sons of her first cousins. Daniel Billings and Ebenezer Edwards later married her nieces, the daughters of her brother.

LXVIII. [verse 721] Ebenezer Tucker Jr., son of Ebenezer Tucker Sr. and Elizabeth Atherton, Born 10 May 1765, Milton MA, Died 26 September 1775, Milton MA. He was the great-great-grandson of John Fenno. (ref. "Index to Revolutionaries," in *"Birth and Shipping Records,"* op. cit., p. 295)

His siblings were John Tucker, Born 4 January 1767, Atherton Tucker, Born 24 July 1768, and Elizabeth Tucker (born 6 April 1772). He died before the others were born.

His father was Ebenezer Tucker, son of William and Rachel Tucker, Born 5 December 1729, Milton MA.

LXVIII. [verse 722] Ref. "Muster-Roll of Capt. Ebenezer Tucker's Company of Militia in Milton, that traveled eight miles from and eight miles to their homes in consequence of the alarm on the 19 of April, 1775, and served in the defence of the Colony against the Ministerial troops before the Standing Army was completed." (ref. "Lexington Alarm," in *The History of Milton, Mass. 1640 to 1887,"* edited by A. K. Teele, 1887, p. 430)
https://archive.org/details/historyofmiltonm00teel/page/430

LXVIII. [verse 724] ref. *"Massachusetts Soldiers and Sailors in the War of the Revolution,"* Wright & Potter Printing, Boston, 1896-1908, Vol. 16, Page 100. There are separate entries for "Tucker, Ebenezer, Milton. Captain of a Milton co. of militia," and for "Tucker, Ebenezer, Jr., Milton. Private, Capt Ebenezer Tucker's (Milton) co. of militia." Both entries state: "which marched in response to the alarm of April 19, 1775; service, 7 days, before completion of the standing army; reported returned home."

LXVIII. [verse 724] Maps drafted c. 1775 (see last page in this volume) show the narrow land bridges connecting Boston and Charlestown to the mainland of Massachusetts (before the Back Bay was filled in and claimed from the sea), thus making it easy to trap the British troops. For example:
https://collections.leventhalmap.org/search/commonwealth:3f462w00z
https://collections.leventhalmap.org/search/commonwealth:z603vr778
https://collections.leventhalmap.org/search/commonwealth:st74cw36c

LXVIII. [verse 725] My own ancestor's brother, Solomon Curtis of Salisbury, Connecticut, enlisted at age eleven with his father, John Curtis. (ref. Deposition of Asahel Curtis, aged eighty-four, 28 May 1850, in Pension Case for Hannah Taylor, widow of Solomon Curtis, Image 90)

LXVIII. [verse 726] "Ebenezer son of Mr. Ebenezer Tucker & Elizabeth his wife he Died Sept. 26 1775 Aged 10 Years & 4 Months." (see photograph of his gravestone at Milton Cemetery, www.findagrave.com)

EPILOGUE

LXIX. [verse 729] Most of the early court order books from colonial Virginia have indeed been transcribed, word for word. Another ten court order books from five Virginia counties are on microfilm. Most of those from Maryland have not been transcribed. Those from Charles County are on microfilm. Sixty-nine original court order books from Maryland, neither transcribed nor microfilmed, were examined by this author for compilation of his books. A full accounting is presented in *"Without Indentures,"* op. cit., pp. xxv-xxviii.

LXIX. [verse 732] A table of the annual breakdown of white slave children brought to court is presented in *"Without Indentures,"* op. cit., p. xiii.

LXIX. [verses 733-736] ref. *"Emigrants in Chains: A Social History of Forced Emigration to the Americas of Felons, Destitute Children, Political and Religious Non-Conformists, Vagabonds, Beggars and Other Undesirables,"* by Peter Wilson Coldham, Genealogical Publishing Company, Baltimore, Maryland, 1992.

LXIX. [verses 734-735] The long title was: "An Act for the further preventing Robbery, Burglary, and other Felonies, and for the more effectual Transportation of Felons, and unlawful Exporters of Wool; and for declaring the Law upon some Points relating to Pirates." The law was in effect until 1776 when it was superseded in 1776 by "An act to authorize, for a limited time, the punishment by hard labour of offenders who, for certain crimes, are or shall become liable to be transported to any of his Majesty's colonies and plantations." The full texts can be found in *"The Statutes at Large from the Magna Charta, to the End of the eleventh Parliament of Great Britain,"* [continued to 1806], by Danby Pickering.
See also https://en.wikipedia.org/wiki/Transportation_Act_1717 and www.encyclopediavirginia.org/Convict_Labor_During_the_Colonial_Period

LXIX. [verse 737] "He has constrained our fellow Citizens taken Captive on the high Seas to bear Arms against their Country, to become the executioners of their friends and Brethren, or to fall themselves by their Hands."

LXX. [verse 738] Impressment of sailors was first made lawful by Queen Elizabeth in 1563, though drafting of soldiers had been a common practice dating back to the thirteenth century. (ref. *"British Navy Impressment,"* at www.pbs.org/opb/historydetectives/feature/british-navy-impressment)

LXX. [verse 738] British naval vessels would stop American ships to search for English crewmen. American sailors who could not prove their citizenship were often impressed into service. (ref. *"Prelude to the War of 1812,"* at https://www.marinersmuseum.org/sites/micro/usnavy/08/08a.htm)

LXX. [verse 739] ref. *"Prelude to the War of 1812"* and *"British Navy Impressment,"* op. cit.

LXX. [verses 740-742] ref. *"British Navy Impressment,"* op. cit.

LXX. [verse 743] Nine thousand men is the smallest number I could find. According to *"British Navy Impressment,"* op. cit., it was fifteen thousand.

LXX. [verse 744] According to the third United States Census, conducted on 6 August 1810, there were 7,239,881 people living in the United States, of which 1,191,362, or 16.45%, nearly one in six, were slaves.

LXXI. [verses 746-747] The full text of the "Corner Stone" Speech of Alexander H. Stephens (Savannah, Georgia, 21 March 1861) is presented at http://teachingamericanhistory.org/library/document/cornerstone-speech

See also *"Slavery and the Civil War,"* National Park Service, at www.nps.gov/liho/planyourvisit/upload/cw_slavery_site_bulletin.pdf

LXXI. [verse 750] It is often stated that only 5% to 6% of the southern households owned Negro slaves. These numbers were derived from the United States Census of 1850. In the fifteen slave states (including Delaware, Maryland, Kentucky, and Missouri), the free population was 6,412,605, of whom only 347,525, or 5.42%, were slave holders. But this is not the proper comparison, and it is therefore misleading. The persons identified in the census as slave holders were heads of households. In the fourteen slave states for which data are available, there were 5,817,983 free persons living in 1,010,764 households (5.756 free persons per household). Thus it can be fairly estimated that 31.2% of the free households owned Negro slaves.

LXXI. [verse 751] ref. *"Civil War on the Western Border, 1854-1865,"* by Jay Monaghan, University of Nebraska Press, 1984.

LXXI. [verses 753-755] The full text of Abraham Lincoln's first Inaugural Address is presented at https://www.bartleby.com/124/pres31.html

LXXI. [verse 756] The price in 1850 of an able-bodied male slave in his early twenties was about $800 (ref. https://eh.net/encyclopedia/slavery-in-the-united-states) According to the United States Census of 1860 there were 3,950,511 Negro slaves. The final official estimate of the cost of the Civil War was $6.19 billion dollars (ref. https://civilwarhome.com/warcosts.html)

LXXI. [verse 757] First Debate with Stephen A. Douglas, Ottawa, Illinois, 21 August 1858. Definition of Democracy, Springfield, Illinois, 1 August 1858, cited in *"Collected Works of Abraham Lincoln,"* Roy P. Basler, ed., Rutgers University Press, New Brunswick, New Jersey, 1953, Vol. 2, Page 532. Speech on the Kansas-Nebraska Act, Peoria, Illinois, 16 October 1854.

LXXI. [verse 758] Letter to Horace Greeley, 22 August 1862 (ref. http://www.abrahamlincolnonline.org/lincoln/speeches/greeley.htm)

LXXI. [verse 759] Thirteenth Amendment to the United States Constitution.

LXXI. [verse 760] The full text of Abraham Lincoln's second Inaugural Address is presented at https://www.bartleby.com/124/pres32.html

LXXII. [verses 761-765] *"Kidnapped,"* by Robert Louis Stevenson, 1886.

LXXII. [verses 766-767] *"Kidnapped,"* starring Warner Baxter and Freddie Bartholomew, directed by Otto Preminger, Twentieth Century Fox, 1938.

LXXII. [verses 768-769] The Motion Picture Production Code, as first enumerated in 1927, included these points: "Resolved, That those things which are included in the following list shall not appear in pictures produced by members of this Association, irrespective of the manner in which they are treated: 5. White slavery;" "And be it further resolved, That special care be exercised in the manner in which the following subjects are treated: 2. International relations (avoiding picturizing in an unfavorable light another country's religion, history, institutions, prominent people, and citizenry);" ref. https://en.wikipedia.org/wiki/Motion_Picture_Production_Code

LXXIII. [verses 770-775] *"The curious origins of the 'Irish slaves' myth,"* by Natasha Varner, Public Radio International (PRI), 17 March 2017. (ref. https://www.pri.org/stories/2017-03-17/curious-origins-irish-slaves-myth)

"Debunking a Myth: The Irish Were Not Slaves, Too," by Liam Stack, The New York Times, 17 March 2017.
(ref. https://www.nytimes.com/2017/03/17/us/irish-slaves-myth.html)

LXXIII. [verses 775-776] ref. *"Without Indentures,"* op. cit., p. xiii, citing "Calendar of State Papers Colonial, America and West Indies, Volume 1: 1574-1660," W. Noel Sainsbury (editor), published 1860, pp. 407-409, 6 September 1653, and pages 431-432, 3 October 1655. Orders of the Council of State.
http://www.british-history.ac.uk/report.aspx?compid=69274
http://www.british-history.ac.uk/report.aspx?compid=69297

LXXIV. [verses 784-800]

Channing, Edward, *"A History of the United States, Volume II, A Century of Colonial History, 1660-1760,"* The MacMillan Company, New York, 1908.

Adams, James Truslow, *"The March of Democracy: The Rise of the Union,"* Charles Scribner's Sons, New York and London, 1932.

Huberman, Leo, *"We, the People,"* with illustrations by Thomas Hart Benton, Harper & Brothers Publishers, New York and London, 1932.

Calverton, V. F., *"The Awakening of America,"* The John Day Company, New York, 1939.

Morison, Samuel Eliot, *"The Oxford History of the American People,"* Oxford University Press, New York, 1965.

The relevant passages are abstracted in "What the History Books Used to Say," in this volume.

LXXV. [verses 807-808] "In 1671 Laurence Trent, merchant, and Captain John Guthrie, skipper of the *Ewe and Lamb,* petitioned the Privy Council of Scotland for a license to transport vagabonds to America. A ship of that name was searched at Leith in 1668 because it was believed to have aboard a number of people who had been kidnapped and were being transported against their will. In 1673 Maurice Trent, merchant in Leith, co-owner of the *Hercules,* under master Andrew Malloch, also petitioned for vagabonds for Virginia. The Trents seem to have been engaged in shipping children, some unwillingly, to America. James and Maurice Trent, sons of William Trent in Inverness and nephews of Maurice Trent in Leith, settled in Philadelphia, Pennsylvania, before 1681; they imported from Scotland several consignments of children who were sold off as indentured servants in Pennsylvania, particularly in Chester County, during the 1690s." (ref. "East New Jersey and the Delaware Valley," in *"Scottish Emigration to Colonial America, 1607-1785,"* by David Dobson, University of Georgia Press, 1994, op. cit., p. 52).

LXXV. [verse 808] "John Macdonah, servant to Col. George Reade, Esq., imported in the *Ewe & Lamb,* is adjudged to be 16 years old and is to serve until he is 24." (ref. York County, Virginia Records, 24 May 1667, cited in *"Without Indentures,"* op. cit., p. 215).

WHAT THE HISTORY BOOKS USED TO SAY

Channing, Edward, *"A History of the United States, Volume II, A Century of Colonial History, 1660-1760,"* The MacMillan Company, New York, 1908.

Negro slavery played little part in the earlier days; but as the eighteenth century advanced, the employment of negroes became more and more marked in every decade. In the earlier time, white persons bound to service for a term of years [1] performed the hard work of field, forest, and farm, and there were also domestic servants who worked for a weekly wage. (p. 367)

Of the indentured servants, the most interesting were the free willers or redemptioners, who sold their services for a limited term, generally five years, to provide their own passage money or the price of transportation of those who were dependent upon them; among these were the Germans who came to Pennsylvania in the middle of the (eighteenth) century. Otherwise, the great mass of the servants in the colonies were English men, women, and children who had been forced to emigrate by the government or by kidnappers and hard-hearted kinfolk; for these, servitude was little removed from slavery. (p. 368)

Kidnapping, or "spiriting," was at its height in the reign of the second Charles, but it continued long after the death of that monarch. Most of the victims of the "spirits" were boys and girls, who were gathered from the streets of London and Bristol and from the country round about. Usually they belonged to the poorer classes, but sometimes spiriting was made use of to extort money. In 1670 as many as ten thousand persons were spirited from England in one year. [2] A kidnapper stated in 1671 that for twelve years past he himself had annually sent five hundred persons to the colonies, while another declared that he had sent eight hundred and forty in a single year. [3] The records of the London courts give specific examples. [4] (p. 369)

---

[1] These were indentured or indented servants, so called from the name of the contract. They were of various classes, -- free willers, redemptioners, convicts.

[2] Morgan Goldwyn's *"The Negro's & Indian's Advocate,"* 171.

[3] *"Calendar of State Papers, America and West Indies, 1675-1676,"* p. 521.

[4] *"Middlesex County Records,"* iv (index under "Spiriting" and Preface, pp. xii-xlvii. See also "Calendar of State Papers, America and West Indies, 1661-1668, pp. 98, 220, 233, 555.

WHAT THE HISTORY BOOKS USED TO SAY

From *"Calendar of State Papers, America and West Indies: Supplementary Addenda, 1655-1674,"* pp. 516-524, as referenced by Edward Channing.

1671 Jan., Feb.

1214. Affidavits of Mary, wife of Mark Collins, and Thomas Stone against William Haverland, "generally called a spirit." Also of William Haverland against John Steward for spiriting persons to Barbadoes, Virginia, Jamaica, and other places for twelve years, five hundred in a year as he has confessed. Also against William Thiene who in one year spirited away 840, Robert Bayley "an old spirit who hath no other way of livelihood." and others, spirits, Also of Grifith Jones against Mark Collins, a spirit, of Joshua Pretty, and Martha wife of William Tanner. Annexed,

1214. i. Copy of the Act to prevent stealing and transporting other children, passed 18th March 1670[-71]. See Commons Journal, p. 142. [Trade Papers, Vol. CXXIV., pp. 13-18.]

From *"Middlesex County Records,"* as referenced by Edward Channing. Cited previously in this work under "Indictments for Kidnapping" with thirty-nine additional entries. https://search.ancestry.com/search/db.aspx?dbid=61473

25 September 1684 -- True Bill: Jane Price assaulted Richard Jackson and unlawfully put him aboard The Jeofferey with intent to convey him to Virginia.

26 September 1684 -- True Bill: Mary Gwyn and Thomas Black assaulted Alice Deakins and put her aboard The Concord, with intent to transport her to Virginia.

* * * * *

Adams, James Truslow, *"The March of Democracy: The Rise of the Union,"* Charles Scribner's Sons, New York and London, 1932.

Indentured servants, who were of considerable importance in our history, were of all grades. Some came from jails but that means little as in that day men were imprisoned in England for very minor offences and even trifling debts. Under an indenture, men, women, and children were sold or sold themselves into service in the colony for a term of years, -- two or three up to seven or more, -- to pay for their passage. Their term of service completed they could claim land and start life afresh in the New World. Under the strain of the mal-adjustments in the economic condition of England, many of good standing at home took advantage of this way of making a new beginning, and the word servant, which

WHAT THE HISTORY BOOKS USED TO SAY

covered schoolmasters, younger sons of good families, and others, is misleading. It meant merely in many cases those who sold themselves into service in exchange for the costly voyage to America which they could not otherwise pay for. As the trade became organized, wicked ships' captains began to kidnap boys and girls on the streets and sell their time in America. (pp. 12-13)

* * * * *

Huberman, Leo, *"We, the People,"* with illustrations by Thomas Hart Benton, Harper & Brothers Publishers, New York and London, 1932.

Up to this point, you have read about people who were attracted to America for one reason or another and came of their own free will. There were others who came not because they wanted to, but because they had to.

In the early days when America was a colony of England, that country saw a chance to get rid of people who seemed to be "undesirable." Accordingly, hundreds of paupers and convicts were put on ships and sent to America. Some of the latter were real criminals, but many had been put into prison for small offenses such as poaching, or stealing a loaf of bread, or being in debt. However, they were not "good citizens" as far as England was concerned, so what better idea could that country have than to get rid of them? Off to America, whether they liked it or not!

You remember about groups of people that wanted to come but didn't have their passage money, and how they sold themselves, became "bonded servants" for five, six, or seven years just to pay their way across (and a horrible trip it was, too). There were many other "bonded servants" "who were carried here against their will – hustled on board ships, borne across the sea, and sold into bondage. . . . The streets of London were full of kidnappers – 'spirits' as they were called; no workingman was safe; the very beggars were afraid to speak with anyone who mentioned the terrifying word 'America.' Parents were torn from their homes, husbands from their wives, to disappear forever as if swallowed up in death. Children were bought from worthless fathers, orphans from their guardians, dependent or undesirable relatives from families weary of supporting them." (pp. 15-16) [5]

---

[5] Citing Beard, Charles A., and Mary R., *"The Rise of American Civilization,"* one volume edition, pp. 103, 104, MacMillan Company, New York, 1930.

WHAT THE HISTORY BOOKS USED TO SAY

Beneath (the free laborers) were the indentured servants. Their happiness during their term of service depended on the type of master they had. Some were fortunate in getting kind masters who didn't work them too hard and perhaps even helped them get a good start when their term was over. But from the great number of advertisements for runaway servants that appeared in the newspapers we are led to believe that indentured servants had a very hard time. The master might whip them whenever he liked; he might give them the shabbiest clothes and the poorest kind of food; he could say whether or not they might be, married; while they were in his service they were no better than slaves. Some servants were even branded by their masters. If they ran away and were caught they might have to serve five days for every one they had been gone – this in addition to a terrible beating. Some of the indentured servants worked very hard, were fortunate, and went step by step up the scale until they became wealthy landowners. But the majority of them had no such luck. At the end of their terms they were given a suit of clothes, some corn, and a few tools. They faced a hard life. Most of them left for the back country where land was cheap. Many of their descendants are today in the hills in the South, living miserable, poor, ignorant lives, just managing to keep from starving. They live on what they raise, shoot, or steal. They might have been better off if Negro slavery in the South had not made it a disgrace for white people to do field work. **These people are today called "poor whites" and "hill-billies."** (pp. 54. 56)

* * * * *

Calverton, V. F., *"The Awakening of America,"* The John Day Company, New York, 1939.

It is customary to think of slavery in America in terms of the Negro, but slavery here has been white as well as black. Black slavery differed from white slavery mainly in regard to duration. In the beginning, to be sure, many Negro slaves were bound only by the laws of indenture and were allowed their freedom after they had worked out their time of service. These emancipated Negroes were free to buy property, purchase servants and slaves of their own, and were entitled to all the laws of protection possessed by the white freemen of the colony. It was not until after 1640 that life-long slavery of the Negroes became an established and unalterable custom. (p. 257) [1]

In an interesting letter, written as late as 1792, we discover a revealing picture of what the indentured servants had to endure:

WHAT THE HISTORY BOOKS USED TO SAY

Negroes being a property for life, the death of slaves in the prime of youth or strength is a material loss to the proprietor; they are, therefore, almost in every instance, under more comfortable circumstances than the miserable European, over whom the rigid planter exercises an inflexible severity. They are strained to the utmost to perform their allotted labour; ... they groan beneath a worse than Egyptian bondage. (p. 259) [2]

The indentured servant was not viewed as a human being with rights inherent in his own personality; he was part of an estate. In an act passed in 1711, for instance, it was definitely stipulated that all indentured servants should continue to work out their period of servitude even after the master who had bought them had died. (p. 260)

When there were not enough free people to venture voluntarily into the new world under such a condition of servitude, and there were not enough felons to fill the quota, the companies and their captains resorted to either kidnapping or child seduction. Kidnapping was a familiar procedure; in fact, it became so lucrative a business that the court ladies and noblemen found it a most profitable investment. The technique of attracting children into the holds of ships with all variety of false promises became a subtle and sinister occupation. (pp. 261-262)

Edward Neill tells how one hundred children were sent over by the London Company itself upon one occasion, and how the next spring one hundred more were demanded. **The boys became indentured servants, or "apprentices" as** they were euphemistically described, until twenty-one years of age, and girls till the same age except in cases in which they, married earlier. Since the majority of the children shipped over or kidnapped were about twelve years of age, they had to serve approximately nine years of hard servitude. The traffic in maidens at the time became so horrifying that, in one parish alone, forty young girls fled from their homes and hid themselves in out-of-the-way places where they could not be traced and captured. (p. 262)

* * * * *

WHAT THE HISTORY BOOKS USED TO SAY

Morison, Samuel Eliot, *"The Oxford History of the American People,"* Oxford University Press, New York, 1965.

Servants in Maryland – and the same is true of all English and Dutch colonies – might be of any class, from poor gentleman to convicted felon. The average servant was a respectable young person who wished to better himself in the New World but could not afford the cost of outfit and passage. During the four or five years he worked for his master, he became acclimated, learned how to grow tobacco and corn, and in many instances learned a trade. Some maidservants were employed in the manor house; others were dairy maids or worked hoeing tobacco alongside the young men. During the term of service the servant received only food and clothing; but at the end, each was entitled by Maryland law and custom – more generous than those of other colonies – to fifty acres of land, [1] a complete suit of clothes, an axe, two hoes, and three barrels of corn. The former servant could then set up as a yeoman farmer, vote, and even be elected to the assembly. (p. 82)

Next below these respectable members of the servant class were ex-rebels, kidnapped persons, and convicts. James I began, and Oliver Cromwell and the later Stuart kings continued, the business of transporting to the colonies Scottish and Irish prisoners taken in the civil wars, and this practice continued until after the Rebellion of 1745. Most of these unfortunates were sent to the West Indies, where their descendants form a distinct class to this day; but some went to Virginia, Maryland, and New England. From the earliest times a class of London crooks specialized in "trepanning," kidnapping boys and girls. They were "spirited" on board a colony-bound ship, whose master sold their services on arrival to recoup himself for the cost of transport and the kidnapper's fee. (pp. 82-82)

---

[1] In 1663, Maryland repealed "that Clause Injoyning fifty Acres of Land to be allowed to Servants att the end of his or her or their Service" – *"Proceedings and Acts of the General Assembly, January 1637/8-September 1664,"* Volume I, Page 496, Sept.-Oct. 1663, cited by Richard Hayes Phillips in *"Without Indentures: Index to White Slave Children in Colonial Court Records,"* Genealogical Publishing Company, Baltimore, Maryland, 2013, p. xxiv.

* * * * *

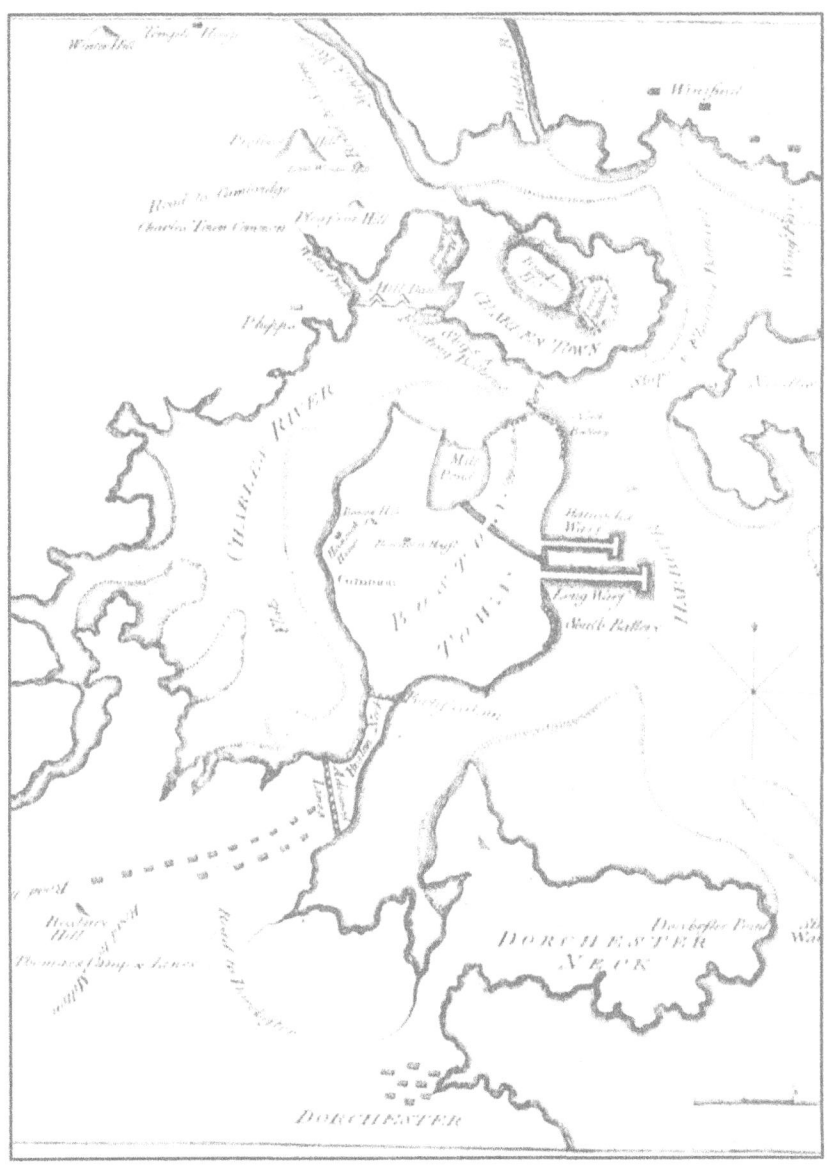

"Map of the Environs of Boston, Drawn at Boston in June 1775," cropped for scale, showing the narrow land bridges connecting Boston and Charlestown to the mainland of Massachusetts (before the Back Bay was filled in and claimed from the sea), thus making it easy to trap the British troops.